Sonata Form

An Introduction

Cecil Hill

Detselig Enterprises Limited
Calgary, Alberta, Canada

Cecil Hill
The University of New England
Armidale, N.S.W., Australia

Canadian Cataloguing in Publication Data

Hill, Cecil, 1936-
  Sonata form
  Includes index.
  ISBN 0-920490-70-0

  1. Sonata – 18th century.   I. Title.
ML1156.H54 1987   781.5'2   C87-091239-9

© 1987 by Detselig Enterprises Limited
P.O. Box G 399
Calgary, Alberta, Canada T3A 2G3

Printed in Canada   SAN 115-0324   ISBN 0-920490-70-0

To
Cedric

in memoriam

for what you taught me

Contents

Detselig Enterprises Ltd. appreciates the financial
assistance for its 1987 publishing program from

Alberta Foundation for the Literary Arts
Canada Council
Department of Communications
Alberta Culture

Preamble

The student who sets out to study the music of the hundred years from c. 1725 to c. 1825[1] must have two objectives. The first is to recognize style in order (a) to be more responsive to the music when heard, and (b) to understand better the spirit of the age in which it was written. The second is to acquire a knowledge of how the style evolved.

Ideas about sonata style have changed over the two hundred years since the writings of Johann Georg Sulzer, Heinrich Christoph Koch, A.F.C. Kollmann, Daniel Türk and others in the late eighteenth century – writers who were usually wise and sound, if very simplistic. The rather rigid views of such later nineteenth-century writers as A.B. Marx, Carl Czerny and Ernst Pauer through to Henry Hadow and Stewart Macpherson were strongly contradicted by such twentieth-century writers as Donald Francis Tovey, R.O. Morris and Cedric Thorpe Davie; though how effective they were in repairing the damaging effects on musical pedagogy of their predecessors is still hard to assess. During this century, a variety of methodologies have been developed to answer some of the complex questions about the nature of musical structure and design, methodologies which have enjoyed greater or lesser degrees of approval.

The intention of this book is to guide the student as thoroughly as possible towards an understanding of the style of late eighteenth century music[2], and particularly that form known as *sonata form*, or *sonata-allegro form* or *first-movement form*.[3] Of course, during the hundred years of its progress there were radical changes; yet there were underlying principles. Any study must attempt to grasp both these principles and the development of their interpretation.

---

[1]The intention here is to discuss sonata style and not that music which is the culmination of technique forged earlier; i.e. the music of the Bach-Handel generation. Furthermore, the term 'classical' is not used in this book, since its use to describe this period is quite mistaken.

[2]The 'eighteenth century' in music is the period from about the mid 1660s to about the mid 1820s. The early eighteenth century embraces the style that culminated in Bach and Handel's generation, the late eighteenth century in Beethoven and Schubert's.

[3]This book is not concerned with the less complex manifestations of sonata style found in the minuet-and-trio. They belong more to the forms categorized as period structures, even though it is sometimes difficult to draw a line between the more complex examples and sonata form proper. Those who grasp what this book hopes to make clear will understand the rest.

To combine a study of underlying principles with the historical development of their interpretation presents the student with a difficult task. However, it can be made easier by recognizing that music is a form of knowlege; and like all knowledge it is subject to modification at any time through both the discovery of new knowledge and the recognition that old knowledge, while still accurate and possibly occasionally useful, is no longer significant or relevant. A study of sonata style shows this to be so. The general characteristics of the style changed as composers discovered new types of texture and theme or that certain tonal manoeuvres were possible.

In any study terminology is a vital factor in the communication of ideas. Much terminology in discussions of music is seriously weak and sometimes downright misleading; it is not good enough to play Humpty Dumpty and say that terminology means what the writer wants it to mean. In this book terminology which has found a secure place in discussions of sonata style has been retained. However, it has been found necessary to introduce some new usage, whose logic it is hoped commends it.

Of course, this book attempts to convey what the writer believes the student should come to know, and the way in which the student ought to approach it. But as there is, from the student's point of view, no limit to the amount of music available for study, the topic can be approached in a spirit of open-ended enquiry. To assist that approach, exercises that should enable the student to consolidate and enlarge on the study are suggested at appropriate points in the narrative. Even so, some students will need the close supervision of their tutors in carrying out the specified tasks, especially those of the first two chapters. While undertaking them, it would be worth remembering that even the great composers wrote certain examples that illustrate better than others of theirs the important points that need to be grasped, and that there is nothing so instructive as comparing examples of different worth to make things clear.

It is assumed that two conditions will prevail for anyone using this book: (i) that a study of basic harmony has already been completed or is in progress; and (ii) that there is ready access to a library that holds enough editions of the repertoire being discussed.

Finally, it must be emphasized that no amount of theoretical study of music will ever give a complete understanding of the topic; careful listening to live performances or recordings is indispensible.

This book took its draft shape from a set of lectures given to the students of the Musikwissenschaftliches Seminar der Westfälischen Wilhelms-Universität Münster, based on ideas I had previously worked out on my students in the Department of Music of the University of New England, Australia. I would like to thank them all for their tolerance and support. I would like to thank too Felicity Gray, Frank Gunner, Derrick Hill and Professor George Wuensch for reading the typescript and helping me to eliminate a number of shortcomings and errors.

Cecil Hill
July 1987

Musical matter is the result of combining three basic elements of music: *texture, theme* and *tonality*. To describe what is presented in, say, the opening bars of a movement as a 'theme' is inadequate, since it does not account for the other two equally important elements.

In sonata style there are five types of musical matter: *statement, transition, preparation, development* and *termination*. While each one often occurs closely dovetailed with one of the others, each one serves a different function.

This chapter is devoted to identifying the nature of the elements and the types of musical matter found in sonata style.

A: Texture

Texture is the sum total of the characteristics of the sound reaching the ear, just as in painting it is the sum total of the characteristics of the light reaching the eye. It has a number of possible features, the important ones being:

- monophony / homophony / polyphony
- frequency of notes
- medium / timbre
- tessitura
- dynamics

Monophony is single-line melody. It plays only a small role in sonata style, because it lacks the necessary dramatic potential. On the other hand, a little monophony judiciously placed, such as that in m.22 of the first movement of Beethoven's *Pianoforte Sonata in E major op.14 no. 1,* can be very effective [see *Example I:16*].

The distinction between *homophony* and *polyphony* in sonata style depends somewhat on the strictness with which their customary definitions is applied, and on a recognition that a rapid alternation of the two (especially in the string quartet) often occurs. It might, for example, be asked where the line can be drawn between them at mm.12-17 and 32-37 in the first movement of Haydn's *String Quartet in C major Hob. III:77.*

Example I:1

Example I:2

There may be a certain futility in this question, since it also can be argued that sonata texture is sonata texture, governed by the complex characteristics of its own style and the medium for which it is written; and because the terms homophony and polyphony have only limited real relevance to it.

The *frequency of notes* is determined partly by the denominations of the notes and partly by the composer's tempo. The performer's own metronome mark is a subsidiary factor. There is, too, a different effect arising from sixteenth notes that are scalic and those that are tremolo.

The *medium of performance* and its use inevitably affects the characteristics of the texture. First is the density and timbre of the instrumentation; for example, the string quartet compared with the string orchestra, or with a wind quintet. Related to that is the authenticity of the instruments. Beethoven's pianoforte sonatas sound quite different when played on a Broadwood grand of the model Beethoven received from that firm in 1818 in comparison with a late twentieth century Steinway concert grand. And similarly, a small orchestra playing eighteenth century instruments for Haydn's or Mozart's symphonies is in a different world from a twentieth century concert orchestra playing the same works.

The *tessitura* is limited only by the compass of the instruments; the composer may set the notes high, middle or low. Beethoven was fond of the occasional wide separation of the hands in his pianoforte writing. An intense climax can be obtained when they are stretched to the extremities of the keyboard. A number of examples can be found in his late keyboard works.

The composer prescribes all aspects of the texture. However, it is the performer, and only the performer, who determines finally the effect on it of the *dynamics*. It is not only a matter of the degree of loud or soft but also of the gradations between them, the degree of accentuation and the balance of the parts at any point. We can never know in every detail how the composers regarded this matter; yet, it is a crucial component of texture.

Exercise 1

Describe some different types of texture found in one sonata movement for orchestra, one for string quartet and one for pianoforte. Attempt to assess the importance of the different components of the texture in the examples chosen.

B: Theme

A definition of 'theme' is a difficult one to arrive at. Many of those found in textbooks and encyclopedias are dangerously glib. The danger lies in equating 'theme' with 'musical matter,'of which it is only one element. The safe thing to say is that *theme is everything that is not texture or tonality*. These two examples should clarify the point:

i. When musical matter is notated regardless of the medium for which it is written, it becomes separated from its natural texture. The fact that it acquires a new texture is a red herring. Any orchestral piece written on two staves for keyboard is deprived of much of its effectiveness. The Scherzo of Beethoven's Second Symphony would suffer particularly.

Example I:3a

Example I:3b

ii. While it is impossible to give a theme without its tonality,the reverse is possible through a graphic representation of its harmonic structure and key relationships, as is common in Schenkerian analysis. This example is of mm.156-174 of the first movement of Beethoven's *Pianoforte Sonata in C major op.53.*

Example I:4a

Example I:4b[1]

The *components of theme* are melody, rhythm and harmony.

Melody is a series of pitches having temporal rhythm (free or metrical), regardless of any chordal support. Eighteenth century theorists recognized two forms of melody, simple and figured.

Simple melody occurs where the melodic progression coincides with the harmonic progression. Examples in sonata style are few, very rarely strict throughout each phrase, usually short-lived and used for a

---

[1]Roger Kamien, Aspects of Recapitulation in Beethoven's Piano Sonatas, *The Music Forum IV;* New York, Columbia University Press (1976) 207.

specific purpose. It has limited usage in sonata-allegro style, because generally it does not lend itself readily to developmental transformation. On the other hand, its usage can be very effective in the total design, such as the one at m.35 of the first movement of Beethoven's *Pianoforte Sonata in C major op.53.*

Example I:5

Figured melody ranges from that which is fairly close to being simple melody – the second group of the first movement of Beethoven's *Pianofort Sonata, op.31, no.1.*

Example I:6

to that in which as many as a third of all the notes are non-harmonic – the beginning of the finale of Beethoven's *Pianoforte Sonata in B-flat major op.22.*

Example I:7

+ = non-harmonic note

A series of pitch figures can give an illusion of a figured melody, as at the beginning of Beethoven's Fifth Symphony.

Example I:8

When the possibility of both simple and figured melody written in conjunct and disjunct motion is considered (not to mention the variety of rhythm and harmony that can be attached), the great variety of melody in sonata style, as in any other style, will be readily appreciated.

Temporal rhythm arising from the mixing of notes of different time-values is an obvious component of theme. It contributes significantly to the character of a melody and thus to the character of the musical matter. There is a second and perhaps more important feature of rhythm and that is *harmonic rhythm*, or its rate of change of harmony. Harmonic, far more than temporal rhythm, can regulate the sense of movement of a piece of music.

A comparison of the openings of the slow movements of Haydn's *Pianoforte Sonata in F major Hob.XVI:23* (1773) and Beethoven's *Pianoforte Sonata in D major op.10 no. 3* (1798) illustrates how Haydn relies on the mixing of different temporal values in the right hand over arpeggiated triplets to sustain the even movement of the first phrase.

Example I:9

In contrast, Beethoven's piece, also in 6/8, begins with such slow harmonic and temporal rhythm that a sense of movement hardly exists at all. With increased harmonic movement as he inflects the phrase towards G minor at m.5 and slight variety in the temporal rhythm, the sense of movement increases rapidly.

Example I:10

While in neither case are the temporal and harmonic rhythm separable from the melodic contour, it is the two aspects of rhythm that together are the most responsible for creating the deep sense of despondency in Beethoven's movement.

The choice of chords that support a melody, at whatever level of the texture it might be placed, is known as the *harmony*. Many a diatonic melody is open to different harmonizations, which inevitably can produce differently characterized musical matter. An obvious example is merely to change from major to minor and then to find that some less-than-satisfactory chords must be replaced. Another is to provide alternative chords, as an examination of almost any two of Bach's harmonizations of the same chorale will make clear.

The harmony of a passage is not a component of texture, but of theme, since it can exist without reference to the texture. On the other hand, what some might call 'accompaniment' is part of texture. The term, though, is a bad one, since it gives that component of the musical matter an unjustifiably inferior status. The harmonization of the first twelve measures of Mozart's *Symphony in G minor K.550* is a good illustration [see *Example III:9*]. Were the viola part played as simple chords on the first quarter note of each measure or as whole-measure chords, it would make the music meaningless. The repeated eight notes provide a part of texture that is something more than harmonization; they contribute significantly to the music's vitality.

Exercise 2

Find and compare a number of examples of simple and figured melody from different decades of the sonata era. In making the comparison try to account for the roles played by the temporal and harmonic rhythm in the musical matter of which they are a part.

C: Tonality

Tonality is generally regarded as being *loyalty to a tonic*. This definition must apply not only to chordal relationships within one key, but to key relationships within the whole of a movement. This is one of the most important aspects of sonata style that must be understood.

The first fundamental question is not so much "What is a key?", but "How many chords are required before a key becomes a key?" A good illustration of this occurs at the beginning of Beethoven's *Pianoforte Sonata in C major op.53*.

Example I:11

The first four measures appear to be in C major and the next three in B-flat major. The chords of the first four measures are only C major in root position (I), G major in first inversion (V^6) and between them the momentary use on the last two eighth notes of m.2 of a major chord to the seventh in third inversion on the supertonic (V^4_2/V), which is the secondary dominant of C major. The B-flat major section is the same, but a tone lower. The question is, "Is either a *key*? or would the term *tonal standpoint* be a better description?" In neither are there enough chords to constitute a real key, as when there are insufficient words to constitute a grammatically correct sentence. Just as a semantic idea can be conveyed through half-statement or allusion, so too can tonality.

Rather than describe either the C major or B-flat major measures here as *in a key*, it would be more meaningful to use the expression *on a tonal standpoint*. And it can be found that the practice of using tonal standpoints like this is rather more widespread in late eighteenth century music than has been stated hitherto. In fact, tonal standpoints are an indispensable feature of the composition of a musically effective sonata style.

Exercise 3

Find and compare some passages in sonata movements that enable one to distinguish between 'in a key' and 'on a tonal standpoint.' If it is possible, find an example that might be regarded as a borderline case.

The kind of tonality found in sonata style is known as diatonic tonality; that is, tonality based on the twelve major and twelve minor keys of the octave. These twenty-four keys have varying degrees of relationship to each other when one of them is the tonic key. The principal division is between the directly related keys and the indirectly related keys. The directly related keys are those based on the primary and secondary triads of the tonic key, when those triads are used as key tonics. All the rest are indirectly related. Thus the directly related keys to C major and A minor are:

Example I:12

III IV V VI VII I ← A minor

C major → I   II   III   IV   V VI

Orthodox modulation can occur between two directly related keys. A modulation between two indirectly related keys can only be aurally convincing when a key that is directly related to both comes between them. Where sonata composers had need to use indirectly related keys to begin sections in close proximity, they mostly resorted to the intermediate direct relationship. However, they sometimes resorted to tonal juxtaposition similar to that found in *Example I:11*, though it occurs only in special circumstances, the conventions of which became less stringent as the sonata period progressed.

The total tonality of a movement is based on a hierarchy of keys, with the tonic at its pinnacle. In very simple movements, at the level of a period structure, the total tonality is usually something like this:

Major Tonic: I ⟶ V ♯ ⟶ II/III/IV/VI

as required and in any order ⟶ I ♮

Minor Tonic: I ⟶ V or III ♯ ⟶ III or V/IV/VI/VII

as required and in any order ⟶ I ♮

In a sonata form movement the tonality is much more complex, largely because of the intricate inter-relationships of the five types of musical matter that will be described in the next section.

> **Exercise 4**
>
> Select a major movement by Haydn, Mozart, Beethoven or Schubert and reduce it to its harmonic essence on a single stave. Note in some way the significant tonal points of the movement.

Having referred to the elements that together form musical matter, the chapter now turns to the types of musical matter.

D: Statement

In language, statement is what sets forth explicitly that which is to be made known. Of necessity it contains no dispute or debate, though one or other may follow. Statement matter in sonata style similarly sets forth explicitly the principal musical matter of a movement. It can occur at any point within the movement and it may be new or old matter according to the needs of the music. Similarly, at any time during a debate new statements may be introduced or old ones reiterated for emphasis.

The one thing that marks out statement matter is the clarity of its tonality; that is, it is not modulatory as in transition, nor mobile as in development, both of which might be analogous to dispute or debate in language.

In sonata style there are different types of statement, such as the alternatim, seriatim, rising sequence, opening herald, various lied forms and period structures. These are only general distinctions, and it must be emphasized that there was much cross-fertilization.

The *alernatim* type occurs widely throughout the sonata period. The opening of the first movement of Mozart's *Pianoforte Sonata in C minor K.457* is one example:

Example I:13

The rising arpeggio is followed by the trill and repeated chords, which rise to a melodic apex on A-flat and the diminished seventh on the leading note, B-natural. The second phrase begins on the rising dominant arpeggio at the lower pitch. The melodic apex does not rise quite as high, and there is a break in the melody of the phrase from B-natural to D in m.6, compared with two E-flats in m.2. Each phrase comprises two contrasting figures *alernatim*.

The *seriatim* type occurs less widely. It comprises several closely-dovetailed fragments of musical matter; the first thirty measures of the finale of Beethoven's Fifth Symphony give a clear example. It is worth noting that fragments *c*, *d* and *e* are each made up from the repetition of a smaller fragment, shortened in the case of *e*.

Example I:14

The *seriatim* type, which is a single statement, must be distinguished from the kind of group made up of a number of short statements. The continuation of *Example I:13* would illustrate that point.

The *rising sequence* is usually only the first few measures of a longer statement, there being a limit to how far a sequence can be continued. The opening of Beethoven's *Pianoforte Sonata in C major op.2 no. 3* is fairly typical of this type.

Example I:15

The melodic outline of the first two measures is sequenced a step higher, though the harmonic sequence is not (and usually would not be) maintained. Then, it is sequenced higher still and repeated to intensify the climax before the cadence of m.8.

The *opening herald* is rarely more than two or three chords. Beethoven's *Eroica* Symphony begins with a particularly terse example, though it is indispensable to a satisfactory start to that work being made. Another that comes into the category of opening heralds is the first measure of the slow movement of Beethoven's *Pianoforte Sonata in B-flat major op.106*. It was added some time after the work had been completed, and its addition persuaded Ferdinand Ries to question Beethoven's sanity. But Beethoven was right, because the measure forms a vital tonal link with the previous movement. The scherzo is in B-flat major and the slow movement in F-sharp minor, which is the enharmonic notation for its theoretically correct key of G-flat minor.

The various lied forms and period structures occur more frequently in slow movements and finales than in sonata allegro. Often they are complete according to what they would be if separated from a larger movement, as in mm.1-16 of the slow movement of Beethoven's *Pianoforte Sonata in F minor op.2 no.1*. Sometimes they are dovetailed closely into what follows, as mm.1-26 of the slow movement of Beethoven's *Pianoforte Sonata in B-flat major op.106*.

Exercise 5

Find and describe some examples of the principal types of statement.

E: Transition

Transition matter occurs where it is necessary to lead away from one statement towards another in a different key. Transition matter serves to undermine the preceding statement in order to accentuate the significance of what follows. It may be derived wholly or partly from the preceding statement or may be entirely new. Crucial to its effectiveness is the way in which the musical matter that begins the transition is broken down tonally and fragmented thematically. Beethoven's two pianoforte sonatas *Opus 14* offer an interesting contrast.

In the first movement of the E major sonata the matter of m.1 is taken up in m.13:

Example I:16

C# minor inflection

→ B major's dominant, pedal

* = Harmonic apex on secondary dominant

+ Second Group

The pedal E is retained. The A-sharp in the second half of m.14 forces a rising chromatic scale rather than the rising interval of m.3; and that rising scale must come to a harmonic apex, as it does on the second half-note of m.16, the secondary dominant of B major. A modulatory transition has occurred and the preparation for B major follows in mm.17-22.

The transition of the first movement of the G major sonata relies first on the shortening of a repeated note, then on a sequence, both over rising broken chords. Both the theme and the texture are new.

Example I:17

The repeated-note figure of mm.8-9 creates a degree of tension that permits it a limited life-span, and it gives way to what is a variant of its appoggiatura. The rising sequence of the latter leads in m.18 through a secondary dominant to the preparation of the dominant key, D major. The rising scale in the bass here and the rising chromatic scale of the E major sonata are a coincidental connection, though both scales contribute to making a climax at the point where the preparation begins.

In both of these examples, tonal change is a prominent feature of the transition matter. In some the leading away from the first statement and the preparation of the next is carried out entirely in the first key, while the burden of the transition is carried by the textural and thematic elements. The second key is then juxtaposed. In the first movement of Beethoven's *String Quartet in C minor op.18 no.4* a dominant preparation is evident in mm.20-25; but, of course, it is the dominant of the tonic key, C minor:

Example I:18

*Italian Aug. 6th as secondary dominant

After the first statement, ending at m.13, a disruptive passage of tonic and dominant chords begins what must be described, musically, as the transition, despite there being no tonal change. Against that is juxtaposed another statement beginning in m.26 on what is the tonal standpoint of A-flat major.

Exercise 6

Find some examples of transition which change the tonality and some which do not. Describe their characteristics and comment on the roles of the texture, theme and tonality. The best area to search is the late music of Mozart and the early music of Beethoven, though other composers of the time should not be neglected.

F: Preparation

Preparation matter occurs where it is necessary to give significance to a succeeding statement. The preparation must end so poised that the statement appears at just the right moment – or musical disaster will ensue. The crux of good preparation is a tonal structure that leaves the listener with the overwhelming desire for the next statement to begin. Often it is a simple chord progression over the dominant pedal preceded by the secondary dominant, as here in the first movement of Beethoven's *Pianoforte Sonata in C minor op.10 no. 1*:

Example: I:19

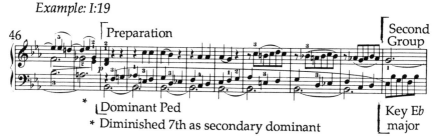

Sometimes it is the alternation of the secondary dominant and dominant chords, ending with the latter [see *Example I:16*, mm. 16ff]. In some cases, especially early in the sonata era, the preparation was no more than the dominant chord of the new key approached through a secondary dominant, as here in the first movement of *Haydn's Pianoforte Sonata in E-flat major Hob.XVI:28*:

Example I:20

In a few special cases the preparation has a more extensive chord progression.

The thematic content of a preparation is often characterized by the repetition of some figure or short phrase. Its purpose is to build a sufficient climax immediately before the entry of the statement. Thematic content may be derived either from old or possibly from the new matter, though it tends to be very nondescript in order not to upstage the subsequent statement.

Exercise 7

Examine the first movement of the first six of Beethoven's pianoforte sonatas or his string quartets *Opus 18* for the way in which he prepares the entry of the second group and the recapitulation.

G: Development

The word development has two applications in music: one is to the second major section of a sonata form movement, the other to a type of musical matter found in that section. As will be explained later, a development section is not always made up entirely of development matter. And there are some development sections without any development matter in them.

The nature of development matter arises from its function, which is to destabilize the music following a period of statement and in anticipation of another significant statement. The intensity of the instability depends partly on the character of the preceding statement, partly on the length to which it is taken, and partly on the capacity of the subsequent statement to confirm a restored stability. Thus, development can be regarded as the antithesis of statement.

The composer faces a difficult task in inventing a type of musical matter that will achieve or maintain a desired degree of instability, while at the same time moving towards the inevitable point of stability provided by the next statement. And where it is necessary to introduce a statement into a long development section, its stabilizing effect must neither impede nor destroy the progress of the music, nor upstage any subsequent statement that must enjoy greater prominence in the totality of the movement.

At the root of the instability of development matter lies harmonic and tonal structure; here, perfect control of the harmonic rhythm is crucial [see p. 13-14]. The kind of chord progression required for a statement (i.e., based on an hierarchical relationship of primary and secondary chords with seventh and chromatic chords being lower in the hierarchy) is not what is required for or found in development matter. Almost the reverse is true. Harmonically unstable chords yielding to other harmonically unstable chords in short sequences that postpone a cadentially formed phrase-ending as long as possible are much more characteristic of development. The following example from the first movement of Beethoven's First Symphony is typical.

Example I:21

Key G major | A major tonal standpoint | Alternating domt.7th/dim.7th | D major standpoint | G major

119

C minor   F minor

The C minor at m.122 is no more than a passing tonal standpoint. In fact, an identifiable key in the sense described above [p. 15ff] is an unthinkable feature of development matter.

Short harmonic periods, and especially those that are treated sequentially, inevitably prevent the use of phrase-structured melody. The consequence must be the fragmentation of the thematic elements of previous statements into their figures or cells. For example, in the third movement of Beethoven's *Pianoforte Sonata in C minor op.10 no. 1* the development matter of mm.46-54 is based entirely on the initial figure of the movement.

Example I:22

The tonality of mm.50-54 passes from E-flat major through F minor (m.52) to the edge of C minor, again as tonal standpoints not keys, with unstable chords made more unstable by the several chromatic appoggiaturas on the half measure in the right hand.

Sometimes entirely new figures are introduced, as with *Figure B* in Example I:21[2]. Sometimes the composer relies on one figure on which to build a substantial portion of the development, as an examination of mm.137-181 of the first movement of Beethoven's Second Symphony will illustrate. At other times figures from different places are joined to form something new, as in the first movement of Beethoven's Eighth Symphony:

Example I:23

---

[2]Some might argue that *Figure B* is a derivative of similar figures in mm.57-58 and 65-66 of that movement, though it would be stretching a point.

In the above example the matter in m.112 made its first appearance in m.96; that in m.108 is a combination of the melody of m.1 and the rocking octave of m.100.

Texture plays an important role in creating the characteristics of development matter. Sharp and rapid contrast of the features described on pp. 7-9 tend to convey a sense of instability; and when combined imaginatively with the thematic and tonal elements, the role of texture can be a most significant one.

Exercise 8

Compare some passages of development matter with the statements from which they are derived, so that the distinction between the two types of musical matter is made clear. Consider particularly the connection between the fragmentation of thematic elements and the chord progression.

H: Termination

A piece of music, and especially a long one, usually does not just end. It is finished off with musical matter that is sufficient in length and appropriate to that function. The composer's objective is to run the movement out with a type of matter that propels the music forward and heightens the effect. To achieve this the music must not introduce such distracting features as general tonal instability or unnecessarily new thematic ideas.

The smallest level on which termination matter usually occurs is the closing measures of the exposition. In mm.41-48 of the first movement of Beethoven's *Pianoforte Sonata in F minor op.2 no. 1* it is a three-times stated four-chord progression below a melodic figure, with the final cadence being prolonged a little.

Example I:24

In the first movement of the third sonata of that set it is rather larger.

Example I:25

A two-measure figure from the middle of m.77 is repeated then extended *forte* into a cadence, from which *fortissimo* broken octave six-teenth notes close into another cadence at m.90. The sixteenth notes go beyond the mere repetition of a cadence formula by adding a vigorous culminating passage.

Both of the above examples are on a simple harmonic level. As the scale of a termination passage increases its harmonic progression may become more varied; but it remains in its tonic key with, at the most, only mild inflexion. This presents the composer with a problem of thematic construction. There are devices the composer can resort to; for example:

i.   extended cadence formulas, often repeated with or without varied texture, and perhaps rhythmically telescoped in order to increase the impetus.

ii. repetition in the tonic key of figures or phrases, even lengthy ones, with or without varied texture. Rhythmic telescoping of the kind found in mm.207-222 of the first movement of Beethoven's *Pianoforte Sonata in E-flat major op.81a 'Les Adieux'* is sometimes employed.

Example I:26

iii.   sequences of any length in the tonic key, though possibly with slight tonal inflection, as in mm.261-273 of the first movement of Beethoven's *Pianoforte Sonata in C major op.53.*

Example I:27

iv.   scalic passage, including broken octaves (or any other interval) of
      the kind described above in Beethoven's *Pianoforte Sonata in C
      major op.2 no 3* (Example I:25),

The test of a composer's technique comes when these devices have to be
drawn on in composing that section of the movement where they are
more likely to appear; namely, the coda. The important test for deter-
mining what termination matter really is, is to listen to it most carefully.

*   *   *

The five distinct types of musical matter described above can be
identified separately within any sonata form movement. But what
makes sonata style so different from any music that had been composed
previously is the way in which these five are closely welded together.
Essential to a real understanding of the essence of sonata style is an
awareness of how that welding is achieved, to which later chapters of
this book are devoted.

2

The Essence of Sonata Style

Tovey described the music of Palestrina's age as "a linked sweetness long drawn out.[1] He went on to observe that Bach and Handel "can visit the same key several times in a composition without inciting the listener to notice the fact either as a purpose or as a tautology." He omitted to mention that with each and every key, however often revisited, went the same theme, with few exceptions. However, it is his word, 'incite,' that is important. Before the appearance of sonata style in the middle of the eighteenth century there was nothing in the style or structure of music about which the word incite might be used. Tovey's next sentence reads, "But Mozart, Haydn and Beethoven build confidently on a knowledge of the exact effect that a modulation in one passage will have on a passage five or even ten minutes later." He could have extended his argument into the combined effect of texture, theme and tonality, though he was discussing only harmony at the time. The word 'incitement' would not have been too strong to use in his description of these composers' purpose.

Tovey's view of the essence of Palestrina's age prompts one to ask whether sonata style might be similarly summarized. Since Tovey was not specific, we might coin the phrase 'the creation and resolution of conflict in music,' because any style that evinces such obvious dramatic characterisitics must depend on factors of conflict, and conflict must at some time be created and then must find some resolution. But what is conflict in music, and how is it created and resolved?

Conflict can be described as any degree of disturbance to the emotional balance of the music arising from the juxtaposition on micro- and

---

[1]Donald Francis Tovey, *Musical Articles from the Encyclopaedia Britannica;* London, O.U.P. (1944) 59. Tovey took these words from line 140 of John Milton's *L'Allegro.*

macro-levels of differing textural, thematic and tonal elements. Of course, there is some degree of conflict in most music; but, unlike the ages of Palestrina, and Bach and Handel, it is the very essence of sonata style. On the other hand, it would be mistaken to assume that every measure or even every phrase in sonata style is riddled with conflict. The issue is one of the calculated use of a stratagem.

In general, conflict is created by transition and development matter and resolution occurs through a statement following a preparation and through termination. To some extent, conflict can exist within preparation, since a preparation always gives a desire for something to follow it; yet, preparation can partially resolve a conflict, especially where the conflict has occurred in development matter. Conflict can also occur within a statement, and does so through the use of contrasting elements.

A: Conflict within Statement

Mozart's *Symphony in C major K.551 'Jupiter'* begins as follows:
Example II:1

⁵ Tonal standpoint
of G major juxtaposed for one measure

F major inflection

The first figure of the statement, with its assertive rising octave triplets *forte (Figure A)*, contrasts sharply with the second figure for the strings alone *piano (Figure B)*; and therein lies the first seed of conflict. The repetition of the two figures beginning on the dominant sharpens the conflict quite markedly, and that must be resolved. The only way Mozart can do this is to continue with an entirely new thematic element (m.9), which, of course, sets up yet another micro-conflict. This in turn is resolved by a short preparation (mm.17-23), which ends on an open dominant note, and the subsequent re-use (m.24) of the first theme with modified texture, which becomes transition matter. In this first statement, conflict is derived from the way in which the textural and thematic elements are structured because the passage is in the tonic key with the exceptions of the briefly juxtaposed dominant tonal standpoint of mm.5-6 and the very slight inflection to F major in mm.10 and 13.

The same sort of conflict can occur with all three elements prominent. At the beginning of Beethoven's *Pianoforte Sonata in C major op.53* the two principal phrases do not juxtapose the tonic and dominant, as in Mozart's *Jupiter* Symphony, but the tonal standpoints of C major and B-flat major.

Example II:2

The first phrase is made up of the contrasting figures *A*, *B* and *C*. Beethoven then juxtaposes the same texture and theme, but beginning with a B-flat major chord. At m.8 the F-major chord is made minor, which allows Beethoven to lead into a preparation for C minor, ending on its dominant at m.13. As the tonic key is major, the mode is turned back to the major at m.14.

By juxtaposing C major and B-flat major, whose relationship is ambiguous, Beethoven sets up a very serious conflict. The only satisfactory way back to C major here is to go via C minor, which is also only a tonal standpoint, then to come to the dominant note of C. The pause is necessary to let the listener's mind clear before proceeding with the first theme in a new texture. Another important factor in this passage is its dynamics. The *crescendo* to *forte*, mm.9-11, helps to diminish the prominence of the B-flat major, and makes the return of C major more easily effected. Here, on the level of a statement with an appended preparation, is an excellent example of Beethoven's methods of creating and resolving micro-level conflict.

Two other ways of creating conflict within statement are 'contrast of tempo' and 'inflection of the key.' Examples of the former are rare, and one of the few is the opening of Beethoven's *Pianoforte Sonata in D minor op.31 no.2*. It also contains 'inflection of the key' and 'tonal juxtaposition.'

Example II:3

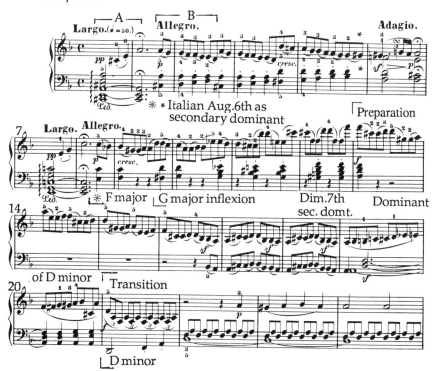

The movement begins *Largo* with an A major chord and a rising arpeggio (*Figure A*). The tonic key is not defined by this; though without prior knowledge one would assume it to be A major. The start of the *Allegro* provides two surprises: one is the new tempo, and the other is the assertion that the piece is in D minor and that it began with the dominant chord. The repeated one-measure figure (*Figure B*) is raised a fourth and the key is inflected towards G minor. The augmented sixth chord (Bb D-G#), functioning as the secondary dominant on the last eighth note of m.5, followed by the dominant chord in m.6 *Adagio*, restores D minor as the tonic. The contrasted tempi, the surprise turn in the tonality, then the key inflection, and the dynamics are all-important to Beethoven's strategy. But the conflict is made even deeper by the start of the next phrase.

The *Largo* returns with a C major chord juxtaposed against the preceding A major chord. This time the information that here is the dominant of F major is more readily accepted, so Beethoven does not need to repeat *Figure B*. Instead he has the greater problem of resolving this further conflict so that the tonic key of D minor can assert itself clearly and so that the movement will not disintegrate into total chaos before it has barely got underway. From F major at m.9, another brief inflection to G minor at m.10 gives the subdominant chord of D minor. It is from this point that Beethoven can now complete the chord progression to lead to a firm preparation. The progression is:

m.10$^{3\text{-}4}$	the neapolitan chord in first inversion
m.11	a leading note (C#) diminished seventh in second inversion
m.12	a diminished seventh on the sharpened fourth (G#) functioning as the secondary dominant
mm.13-20	the dominant pedal (A) over which there is a $^{6\,5}_{4\,3}$ chord progression.

Associated with this chord progression is an all-important *crescendo* [cf. *Example II:2*]; the *forte* at the end of it is maintained into what is the transition at m.21. Here again Beethoven shows his absolute mastery of the art of creating and resolving conflict. Whether, as was claimed by Anton Schindler,[2] Beethoven intended to express sentiments about Shakespeare's *The Tempest* or not is irrelevant to a technical discussion of the passage. What Beethoven does here reveals his thorough understanding of musical knowledge, to the development of which he was making a considerable contribution.

---

[2]Anton Felix Schindler, *Beethoven as I knew him: A biography*, ed. by Donald W. MacArdle; New York: Norton (1972) 406.

This and the other examples of conflict within statement matter that are given above are taken from those that make a lot of the issue. They will be readily appreciated aurally, if found by some to be a little difficult to understand theoretically. There are many others, especially earlier in the sonata style period and among the lighter pianoforte sonatas, that have very little or no conflict within their statement matter. They rely on conflict arising from the contrasting of whole statements and on what can be built into the transition and development matter.

Exercise 9

Find and comment on some examples of statement matter that have readily identifiable features of different kinds that cause conflict. Compare examples from different decades of the sonata style period.

B: Conflict within Transition

The transition matter that is used to lead from one statement (or group of statements in a basic key) to a second statement usually has only one point of conflict. It is that crucial point where *either* the first key begins to break down to make way for the key of the second statement, *or* where there is the sudden intrusion of a new and aggressive theme which retains the tonic key for the preparation, against which the second statement in the new key is juxtaposed.

A comparison of the first statement of the first Allegro of Haydn's *Symphony in G major Hob.I:92 'Oxford'* with the corresponding measures of the transition reveals the critical point of the key change and how he continues so that the key of the second principal statement, D major, can be properly prepared. *Example II:4* lays out the comparable bars as closely as possible.

Example II:4

First Group
Allegro spiritoso.

Domt.7th harmony

Transition

Begins with first phrase.
New texture again *piano*.

Texture only
slightly changed

forte asserts tonic

Tonal conflict

E minor inflection   unsecured D major to m.55

Sec. domt. → secure

No secondary dominant, therefore D major is an inflection

⌐Second Group

D major

The mind might have expected the statement (m.41) to proceed as before, but is surprised by the sudden inflection to E minor at m.47, after which the transition continues with the unsecured key of D major in a manner that sounds like preparation. The preparation is more a thematic one, since the confirmation of D major occurs only at the last moment with the secondary dominant on the third quarter note of m.55; the reason for withholding the confirmation is that the first four measures of the subsequent statement (i.e., the first statement now in the dominant) are harmonized by the dominant seventh.

An example of the use of thematic intrusion as the principal means of creating conflict through transition is given above as *Example I:18*; there are numerous others.

Whatever degree of conflict arises from either the tonally disruptive or the thematically intrusive form of transition, some form of preparation to resolve it usually follows, and only occasionally – as in mm.19-22 of the first movement of Mozart's *Pianoforte Sonata in C minor K.457* – does it not. The transition there is a mere four bars comprising two harmonies, C minor and B-flat major. The former functions as the tonic of C minor and the submediant chord of E-flat; B-flat is the dominant of the latter. The modulation is abrupt and in that is a factor of micro-conflict.

Example II:5

Exercise 10

Find and comment on a number of examples of transition matter with special reference to their degree of conflict. This requires consideration of the role of each of the three elements separately or in combination, and in most cases consideration of the characterisitics of what precedes the transition. It should be noted that transition matter can occur at various places within a movement.

C: Conflict within Development

As was pointed out in *Chapter I*, Section G development matter is made of progressions of unstable chords, short harmonic periods, rapidly successive tonal standpoints, fragmentation of thematic elements (often to build short sequences) and rapidly contrasted texture and theme. These in themselves will be readily detected by the ear as sources of conflict; but used by a master of the art, they can create degrees of intensity that no other type of musical matter can. But conflict within development is a much more complex issue because development matter is confined to the development section of a sonata form movement, which itself is often a deft mixture of statement, transition and preparation as well as development matter. And even these may be made up of new or old textural and thematic elements. Therefore, conflict in development matter must be viewed in terms of what is within itself, as well as the relationships among the four types of matter that can be found in the development section.

Exercise 11

Examine some examples of development matter and attempt to assess the degree of conflict each one creates. At this stage, do not consider the relationships of the different types of musical matter within the development section.

D: Conflict and Resolution within Preparation

Preparation can only lead away from a point of conflict to a point of resolution provided by a statement. It is most unlikely that a preparation in a sonata form movement could ever create a degree of conflict that did not exist immediately before. However, preparation often does retain the intensity of a preceding conflict right up to the beginning of the succeeding statement; Beethoven's music particularly is littered with examples of this kind. However, preparation can also provide a point of partial resolution of a preceding conflict. In the first movement of Beethoven's Fourth Symphony the transition begins at m.81 aiming at the second principal statement in F major at m.107.

Example II:6

m.1 theme new texture

Transition

Tonal conflict

D minor inflection

Dominant of F

F minor to m.102

Preparation
95
sf dimin.
Second Group
106
F is now major
sempre p
F major

The critical point is at m.89, where the key is inflected towards D minor (i.e., VI in F major); but following the diminished seventh as the secondary dominant in m.91, then the dominant seventh in m.92, the mode becomes F minor at m.94, and that persists through the offbeat half-notes of mm.95-102. The minor mode is not retained to the end of the transition. In such circumstances, the major is usually restored discreetly towards the end of the preparation, as Beethoven does in mm.103-106. Thereby, the conflict of the transition is completely resolved, and not made worse by an abrupt change from minor to major as the second group enters.

Exercise 12

Assess the relative degrees of conflict and resolution that can be found in some examples of preparation matter. In each case compare the thematic content with what precedes and follows, and note the form and role of the secondary dominant in the chord progression.

E: Resolution through Termination

The distinction between any passage of termination matter and a passage of development matter is that the latter creates conflict (or intensifies what is already there), whereas the former resolves any conflict. The most important factor in this is the absence from termination matter of anything that is tonally disruptive.

The simplest form of termination matter is a repeated cadence formula, perhaps comprising only the two cadence chords. A more effective kind of termination matter is that which extends some figure towards the final cadence. The coda of the first movement of Beethoven's *Pianoforte Sonata in D major op.28* begins at m.438 with the musical matter of m.1. It is joined to the previous measures in almost exactly the same way as the end of the exposition is joined to its repeat or to its continuation by mm.157-163.

Example II:7

Mm.438-447 are the same as mm.1-10 slightly modified texturally. From m.447 *Figure X* together with a previously unheard upbeat is made the feature of the thrust to the end. By repeating *Figure X* and causing the upbeat notes to rise up the arpeggio, Beethoven forces a climax at m.455 from which he brilliantly terminates the movement by abandoning *Figure X*, continuing with its upbeat, but abandoning its *sf*, making a *decrescendo*, then adding the *pianissimo* cadence. All this is in the tonic key, and except for the last two bars is set over a tonic pedal.

Exercise 13

Compare termination matter as found at the end of a movement with that found at the end of the exposition.

F: Relationships between musical matter

This chapter has referred so far to conflict and resolution within the five types of musical matter. The discussion now turns to the relationships between adjacent musical matter and between and across larger sections of a movement. A very important factor to note is the role of new and old matter, because it is through their proper relationship that the essence of the style is evoked. While this is rather more important with regard to adjacent pieces of musical matter, it also has great significance in the overall structure. To repeat Tovey's point, "Mozart, Haydn and Beethoven build confidently on a knowledge of the exact effect that a modulation in one passage will have on a passage five or even ten minutes later."

When the first statement (in some cases only the first phrase) of a movement has been played, what follows will be old or new in one or more of the texture, theme and tonality. When any subsequent matter is played, it too will have new or old elements, *either* in relation to the first statement *or* to any other musical matter that has preceded it. This table shows that there are eight possible combinations:

	Texture	Theme	Tonality
1.	old	old	old
2.	old	old	new
3.	old	new	new
4.	old	new	old
5.	new	new	new
6.	new	new	old
7.	new	old	new
8.	new	old	old

The immediate and exact repetition of any passage can prove disastrous in sonata style. Even repetition with only the texture changed is often unsatisfactory, because sonata style depends for its success on the variety and organic growth of the musical matter. In other words, it is the proper relationship of new and old matter that is the vital factor of continuity in all diatonic music.[3] Therefore, the first and last of the options in the above table occur very rarely, and only in very special circumstances. Having established that a sonata form movement is a combination of deftly-mixed new and old musical matter, two questions arise: "How are the different types joined together?" and "In what order or by what conventions?"

The order is not in any way determined by texture; rather the reverse. The texture is determined by the other two elements. To some extent the order is determined by the characteristics of the thematic elements, because some theme types are more suitable for a statement in the first principal key than for a statement in the second principal key, and so on. What does determine the order more than anything else is the tonality. In essence, a movement will begin in the tonic key; it will then move to another key which makes what Tovey called "a psychological step up"; then it will digress through other keys and, finally, will come back to the tonic key [see also p. 16]. This fundamental tonal structure is characteristic of all diatonic music. It is the expansion of the fundamental into a complex and refined structure that gives sonata form its endless variety and fascination.

That portion of a sonata form movement containing the musical matter in the first and second principal keys is known as the *exposition*,

---

[3]In fact, one could extend this argument into the micro-structure of diatonic music; but this is not the appropriate place.

and the two key areas as *first group* and *second group*; the digression is known as the *development* section; and the return to the tonic is known as the *recapitulation and coda*. These have been the traditional terms for describing these sections. While reservations about them might be put forward, there seems to be no overwhelming reason to abandon them at present, provided it is clearly recognized that what matters in any critical commentary is the proper identification and explanation of the five types of musical matter described in *Chapter 1*, in the light of the essence of the style described in this chapter.

Since a sonata form movement is long and complex, it is necessary to spread a discussion of the relationships between adjacent musical matter and between and across larger sections over more than one chapter. This is purely for pedagogical convenience and should not distort the fact that a sonata form movement is a totality. Therefore, the traditional division of *exposition, development* and *recapitulation and coda* is adopted in the ensuing chapters.

3

Exposition

A: First Group

The principal function of the first group is to establish the tonic key. That is usually done with a statement which has a neatly-designed phrase structure, is firm and assertive. It begins with a clear tonic harmony (or perhaps a dominant up-beat) and has a chord progression that is (with a few notable exceptions) clearly in the tonic key throughout. It ends *either* with a perfect cadence in the tonic key *or* with its open-ended dominant. Its structure will be one of the types of statement described in *Chapter 1*, or a variant of it, and its texture will be appropriate to the character of the thematic elements.

Most first groups contain one statement. A few contain more than one; this is always the case where a movement opens with a 'herald,' such as at the start of Beethoven's *Eroica* Symphony. It is also the case where new matter is required to maintain the continuity; or to put it the proper way round: some statements are so constructed that they compel new matter to follow in the same key.

The opening of Mozart's *Pianoforte Sonata in C minor K.457* has already been referred to [p. 17] as an example of *alternatim* statement. Having written this, Mozart could not help but continue with entirely new matter, which he bases on a falling chromatic scale over a dominant pedal, which itself gives way to more new matter for the end of the statement.

Example III:1

Each thematic fragment plays an important role in replacing what is immediately preceding, and the whole is shaped to bring about a satisfactory conclusion at m.19. What the *alternatim* statement gives way to could be viewed as a *seriatim* statement, as indeed could the whole of mm.1-18. This is an example of the cross-fertilization of theme types. What it is essential to observe about this particular first group is its micro-structure and its need to introduce new matter at certain points in order to maintain its continuity.

Beethoven's *Pianoforte Sonata in B-flat major op.106* certainly does begin with a three-statement first group. It is a complex one, but it has in it one simple principle. Like the child's toy containing a spring, which when tightened and then released will shoot a projectile, its second and third statements are each put into deep conflict which forces them to be projected into resolution. This simple principle is fundamental to sonata style on both micro- and macro-levels, and a grasp of it should make the complexity of the first group of *Opus 106* crystal clear.

Example III:2

The first four measures sound like a herald; though, unlike most other heralds, they contain a pregnant rhythm that lends itself readily to extensive development (see mm.133-200). Also unlike most other heralds, it is the thematic substance of the transition at m.34/5. The second statement occupies mm.4-17, overlapping the third in mm.17-34; and it comprises a one-measure figure repeated a tone higher, but extended to the fermata on the dominant. The statement is repeated an octave higher. The fermata is avoided so that mm.10^4 – 12^3 can be repeated as mm.12^4 – 14^3, with a further modified repeat from m.14^4 leading to a perfect cadence in the tonic. The third statement begins in m.17 with a two-measure figure repeated in sequence, with the sequence shortened from m.24. It leads to a preparation from m.27.

A multiple statement made up of a series of themes in one key would be tiresome were the whole passage composed with chords drawn only from the central chords of the key. Just as a Rembrandt would never use a flat color over a large area of canvas, but would tint it with streaks of other colors to give it life and make it convincing, so too would a composer add touches of other keys to any lengthy passage in one key to make it lively and convincing. Foreign notes added to a key for inflection must be put in the right places, and the clarity of the key must be confirmed by the end of the passage.

Having stated only the tonic chord in the herald, Beethoven heavily inflects the key in mm.5 and 6. This is orthodox conflict, which must be and is partly resolved by the imperfect cadence and the fermata. The repetition of mm.5-8 is necessary so as not to produce too much diversity and therefore confusion; but it inevitably renews a conflict that must find a more secure resolution. To do that, Beethoven does not cap it with a perfect cadence; instead, he deepens the conflict even further with the varied repetition of mm.10^4 – 12^3. After a hint of a further repetition at m.14^4, which he aborts, he forces the music *crescendo* to an intense climax, which must come to a perfect cadence. In fact, deepening the conflict as in mm.12-15 is Beethoven's only means of resolving it satisfactorily, and the resolution has to be in the tonic key, otherwise mm.4-17 would have had to become the transition.

New matter had to follow at m.17, because of the tonic perfect cadence. Beethoven had two options here. One was to treat the new matter as the start of an expository transition (see below, p.62ff), which would have modulated towards the second principal key. The other was to give a third statement within the first group. In taking the second option, Beethoven had to avoid – even more than before – writing in a 'flat-wash' key to avoid the risk of damaging the musical momentum and the continuity. Again, he resorts to extensive inflection of the key in mm.20-26, and leads that into a preparation, which ends with the broken dominant chord rising through mm.31-34. The *diminuendo* and *ritardando* are interrupted by the herald as it begins the transition.

Exercise 14

Find and examine some examples of multiple statement first group, and attempt to identify the means by which the composer maintains the continuity of the music. There are straight-forward examples among keyboard sonatas and chamber music. A more difficult one to discuss is the opening of Beethoven's *Eroica* Symphony.

Wherever there is to be a conflict, the composer will usually begin a passage in the key of the moment, introduce the conflict after a sufficient number of measures, then resolve it. Questions are, "How soon can a conflict be introduced?", and "Can a piece begin with conflict?" Mozart's *Fantasia in C minor K.475* possibly does; but then it is a fantasia and is permitted almost any licence. The finale of Beethoven's Ninth Symphony certainly does, but that is necessary to justify the words with which the bass soloist begins the vocal section at m.216. But what of a movement in sonata form?

To begin in conflict a movement must start with something other than tonic or up-beat dominant harmony. Beethoven's *Pianoforte Sonata in D minor op.31 no.2* is, for reasons already discussed [p. 42f], one example of a movement beginning in conflict. His next sonata is another. The first movement begins as follows:

Example III:3

Key Eb major

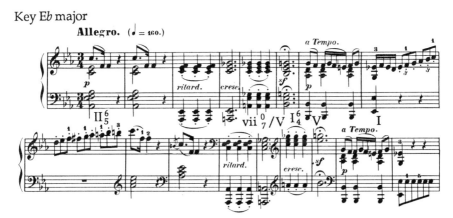

The first chord might seem confusing at first, (probably the reason why almost as much ink has been spilt over it as over the infamous Wagner *Tristan* chord). It is not, as is sometimes stated, an added sixth of the subdominant chord; rather, it is a supertonic seventh in first inversion. The next chord (mm.4-5) is a diminished seventh on the sharpened fourth functioning as the secondary dominant. That is followed by the second inversion of the tonic chord (m.6), then the dominant seventh (m.7) and finally the tonic chord (m.8). The first chord's seventh (E-flat) is held in the alto part until m.7, where it is correctly resolved on to D. The doubling of the seventh in the first three bars is purely textural, and that might be what has caused the confusion.

The progression II $^6_5$ – I $^6_4$ – V – I is perhaps the first lesson every harmony student should be taught after learning what a perfect cadence is, because it is a basic cadential progression of all diatonic music. A glance at Bach's chorale-harmonizations will prove that point. This one is merely enhanced through the addition of the diminished seventh secondary dominant, about which there is nothing abnormal. Therefore, what Beethoven does here is to start in the middle of a normal harmonic progression leading to a cadence. He does so with a firm and assertive figure, even though it quickly loses its force in the *ritardando*. Without doubt he begins in mild conflict, and at the same time invents, along with the previous sonata, a wholly new type of statement and a wholly new approach to beginning a movement.

Exercise 15

While there are only a few movements that begin in conflict (as do *Op.31, no. 2 and no. 3*), attempt to find others. Then come to Beethoven's *Pianoforte Sonata in E-flat major op.81a 'Les Adieux'* and examine the first movement at the join of the *Adagio* and the *Allegro*.

B: The Transition

The function of the transition between the first and second groups is to change the key, so that *either* all sense of the first key is removed and the second key is carefully prepared for, *or* at least the second key can enter with a sense that it is the new tonic. The majority of transitions modulate to the edge of the new key. Some do not; instead they end on the dominant of the first group key, against which the new key is juxtaposed. With either of these tonal processes are associated textural and thematic elements, which may be new or old. A transition never begins in a key other than the key of its preceding passage.

A transition that begins with an entirely new thematic element may be described as *expository*. When it begins with a thematic element that appeared in the first group, it may be described as *derived*. There are a few cases of an expository transition ending with a thematic element derived from the first group. There are also cases of a derived transition introducing new elements. It will be found, however, that all derived transitions modulate to the edge of the second group key; none has yet been found that doesn't. Expository transitions do either; though without a count of a sufficiently large number, it would be hazardous to guess whether the modulatory or the non-modulatory expository transitions are in the majority.[1] Thus there are three basic types of transition to consider: derived; expository/modulating; expository/non-modulating.

i. Derived

Where a transition is derived from first group matter, it begins in the tonic key with the thematic element of the first measure, though with at least slightly, sometimes substantially changed texture. It is often relatively short, with the tonal conflict occurring as soon as possible, then moving quickly to a climax and to the edge of the new key. *Example I:16* is a very clear instance of this approach; and there are many others.

---

[1]It might be reliable to claim that earlier in the sonata period an expository transition usually would not modulate, whereas later in the sonata period more likely it would.

Some derived transitions use more than the thematic element of the first measure. Mozart's *Symphony in C major K.551* actually uses all those of the first group (mm.1-23) for the transition (mm.24-55), which proves to be nine measures longer. Sometimes the derivation is substantially varied. Beethoven's *Pianoforte Sonata in B-flat major op.22* begins with:

Example III:4

but the transition makes a different thematic element out of the sixteenth-note figure.

Example III:5

The relatively long preparation, mm.16-21, is necessary because of the depth of the tonal conflict of mm.13-15, which contains a new thematic element. Strictly, this example belongs among those described below as derived/expository. Conflict is an indispensible component of the transition between the first and second groups, and there are many different ways of creating it. They always come down to the composer's use of new and old textural, thematic and tonal elements.

Sometimes there are inexplicable surprises. Beethoven's *Pianoforte Sonata in F major op.10 no.2* prepares for a second group that might be in A minor or even A major.

Example III:6

Dominant of A ↾ C major

The transition begins in the same way as m.1. Beethoven then moves to the German augmented sixth chord (F-A-C-D#), treats that as the secondary dominant of A minor,[2] then ends on an E major chord in m.18. Instead of going into an A key at m.18/19, Beethoven audaciously but characteristically jumps into C major. This is the key he should have been aiming for in the first place.

ii. *Expository/modulating*

The clever composers knew that some musical matter was suitable for starting movements and other matter was unsuitable. It would be fair to claim that musical matter which was used to begin any expository transition would be unsuitable to start a movement. The reason can be attributed to one or more of the three elements. Apart from that distinction, musical matter that begins a modulating expository transition can be of widely varied character. Some of it, like that of the first movement of Beethoven's *Pianoforte Sonata in A major op.2 no.2*, is that of the urgent transition to the new key.

---

[2]The two orthodox secondary dominant chords in a minor key are the diminished seventh chord on the sharpened fourth (= the secondary leading note) or one of three augmented sixth chords on the sixth of the scale. See: Cecil Hill, That Wagner-*Tristan* Chord; *The Music Review*, 45 (1984) 7-10.

Example III:7

Some, like that of *Example I:17*, can be rather more expansive, and can take some time to come to the tonal change and to complete the preparation. The number of separate pieces of musical matter that might occur in this type of transition depends on the character and structure of the transition itself and on the larger conception of the exposition and the movement. When there is more than one piece of musical matter, such as in the transition (mm.17-46) of the first movement of Beethoven's *Pianoforte Sonata in E-flat major op.7*, they will be associated with the start of the transition, then as at m.25 with the point of tonal change, and with the preparation as at m.35.

Example III:8

The scalic passage mm.17-24 is unmistakably in the tonic, E-flat major. The tonal crisis at m.25 is the *fortissimo* intrusion of the A-flat major tonal standpoint, which is sequenced up to B-flat minor. The German augmented sixth chord – that is, the secondary dominant of that key – precedes the preparation, which itself retains the minor mode.

iii. Expository/non-modulating

This type of transition is in the tonic key throughout, and invariably ends with a dominant preparation preceded by the secondary dominant. Thus, the opportunity for creating conflict through a change in the tonality (always the most effective) is removed. This throws the burden of conflict creation on to the textural and thematic elements.

Most examples of this type begin immediately on the conclusion of the first statement with matter which sounds initially like statement, but is much more urgent in character than the first statement and is usually loud throughout. It is not possible to envisage an example containing more musical matter than the principal one and any extension of it, followed by whatever dominant preparation is necessary. Examples of this type are much more abundant earlier in the sonata period than later. One of Beethoven's more notable ones has been referred to previously as *Example I:18*.

Exercise 16

Find and compare some of the different types of transition, assessing the relationship of each one to other musical matter in the movement, the degree of conflict achieved and how it is created, and the approach to the second group.

There are two extensions of the types of transition described above. They are the *derived/expository* and the *expository/derived* orders of the matter. Both modulate. The reasons for each are usually local. In the former case it can be almost guaranteed that the expository matter will be in the new key. Two well-known examples are worth describing here. The first statement of Mozart's *Symphony in G minor K.550* is:

Example III·9

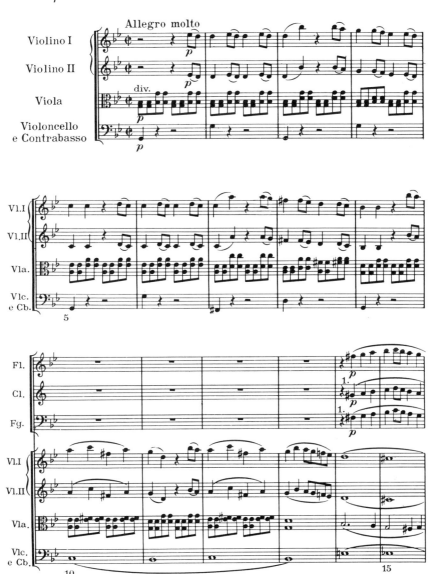

The transition occupies mm.20-42:

Example III:10

The relationship of the transition's first phrase to mm.1-5 is obvious, but there are changes; namely, the postponement of the tonic chord to m.22, the addition of the woodwind and the new harmony in m.24 – the last of these being the most important. Instead of putting the second phrase on the dominant of G minor, Mozart places it on the dominant of B-flat major. This makes the melody higher in pitch than previously, and therefore intensifies the phrase's effect. In bringing about the modula- tion to the second group's key, B-flat major, prematurely, Mozart must introduce a new theme (and texture). He certainly could not have con- tinued with the thematic element of mm.9ff in B-flat major without fail- ing to properly resolve the micro-conflict of the tonal change. This new matter is now treated as if it were a non-modulating expository transi- tion. It proceeds for some measures with quasi-statement, then turns itself into an orthodox preparation for the second group key by laying emphasis on the alternation of the secondary dominant (the diminished seventh chord) and the dominant.

The opening of Beethoven's *Pianoforte Sonata in E-flat major op.31 no.3* is an example of a movement beginning in conflict (see *Example III:3*). The transition begins at m.25.

Example III:11

This kind of trivial scalic and broken chord matter has limited potential in a transition, as Beethoven knew. The way to overcome this shortcoming is to introduce a sharp conflict.[3] The broken chords appear to change the key at m.29, and to include the secondary leading note, E-natural (but not secondary dominant harmony) in m.30. The insistent alternating A-natural/B-flat in mm. 31-32 on a *crescendo* give the impression that perhaps B-flat major will appear via more expository matter. But no! Beethoven arrests the progression with the repeated B-flat *piano* (m.32[6]) followed by the chord of m.33 and a revised version of the musical matter of m.1.[4] The tonal standpoint is E-flat minor, not major, with the harmony II$_5^6$, and it moves to a diminished seventh chord on the leading note on the third quarter-note of m.36. By sequence through mm.39-42 the tonal standpoint is raised to F minor, whose phrase also ends on a leading note diminished seventh.

Beethoven's problem is to get to the real dominant of B-flat. Apart from slight dynamic fluctuations, the first group and transition have remained *piano* throughout. He regards the diminished seventh on the leading note of F minor (m.42) as the secondary dominant of B-flat major. Just to be absolutely sure, he turns it into a German augmented

---

[3]As Beethoven had done previously in similar circumstances in the *Pianoforte Sonata in E-flat major op.7*.

[4]The E-natural (i.e., the sharpened tonic) has now proved to be not the secondary leading note of a B-flat key, but the tertiary leading note of the tonic key. There is such a thing as the tertiary dominant, and it seems it is always the diminished seventh chord on the sharpened tonic.

sixth on G-flat, the flat sixth of B-flat (m.43), then suddenly bangs out the major in the left hand (m.44) and endorses it with falling octaves. The next statement can now occur in B-flat major, and it too is *piano*.

Exercise 17

Examine the first movements of Mozart's *String Quintet in C major K.515* and Beethoven's *Pianoforte Sonata in C major op.53* as examples of the *expository/derived* and the *derived/expository* types of transition.

Traditional methods of descriptive analysis have depended much on answering such a question as, "Where does the transition begin?" Rebels have abandoned this and similar questions, though unwisely. It is a fair question, because the answer can bring both the performer and listener, alike, to a clearer understanding and interpretation of the music. Unfortunately, the answer is too often wrong, even from some of the more eminent analysts. The answer for modulating transitions is simply "from the last main tonic key cadence before the tonal conflict occurs." It cannot begin after the tonal conflict's occurrence. Thus, in *Example III:8* the transition begins at m.17, not as Tovey states at m.25.[5] And in *Example III:11* it begins at m.25 not m.33, where Tovey was misled by the modified version of the m.1 matter.[6]

The answer for non-modulating transitions, all of which are of the expository type, is almost as simple. It begins with the quasi-statement matter preceding the dominant preparation. In *Example I:18* it is at m.13, and the first movement of Beethoven's *Pianoforte Sonata in C major op.2, no.3* it is at m.13.[7]

C: Second Group

Tovey observed that a modulation to the sharp side of the tonality always causes a 'psychological step up,' a modulation to the flat side a 'psychological step down.' This is important for any stage in a sonata form movement; but it is especially important for the second group, whose key is always to the sharp side of the tonic. The second group's function is to exploit that relationship. To do so effectively, its key must assume tonal superiority; to do that the key's identity must be proved; and to do that effectively it must resolve at least one conflict – a conflict that may be solely textural/thematic in the key, or may include tonal conflict as well.

---

[5]Donald Francis Tovey, *A Companion to Beethoven's Pianoforte Sonatas;* London, Associated Board of the Royal Schools of Music (1931) 38.

[6]ibid., 138.

[7]Tovey (ibid. 27) got this hopelessly wrong, strangely for him.

The type of musical matter found in the second group is principally statement; but short passages of preparation are sometimes necessary; and then the group always ends with termination. The character of the statement matter depends partly on the tonal structure of the group and partly on what happened in the preceding transition and sometimes the first group. There are three different basic tonal shapes for the second group:

i. one that is in the principal key throughout, and with possibly only the mildest inflection.

ii. one that is in the principal key, but which has one or more significant conflicts during its course.

iii. one that begins with some form of tonal conflict which later resolves into the principal key for the remainder of the group. (Where the group is long, there may be further tonal conflict in it.)

To illustrate *Shape i* the first movements of Mozart's *Pianoforte Sonata in D major K.311* and Beethoven's *Pianoforte Sonata in C minor op.10 no.1* are worth comparing. Both have expository transitions. Beethoven's modulates; Mozart's doesn't. Both second groups begin with a quiet statement firmly in the key of the group, though they are of a different kind. Mozart's (mm.16-24) is in two phrases of the antecedent-consequent kind, the first ending with an imperfect cadence, the second with a perfect cadence.

Example III:12

Beethoven's comprises a four-measure figure (mm.56-59), sequenced one step up the arpeggio (mm.60-63).

Example III:13

The statement is then repeated using rising scales, merged into a *forte* progression to a cadence (mm.71-76), which is also repeated and then extended through the octave eight-notes of mm.82-86 with the dynamic increased to *fortissimo*. Finally the rhythm of m.1's upbeat is recalled (m.86ff) until a firm cadence is reached at m.94.[8]

Going back to the Mozart example, the end of the first statement at m.24 is abruptly interrupted with the right hand sixteenth notes and its urgent left hand figure. This lasts for only four measures. It is then replaced by a quite different statement, whose phrases are alternately *piano* and *forte* to m.36; mm.36-39 are termination matter. It will be clear that Mozart adds statement to statement, whereas Beethoven allows one phrase to grow out of another; and while not a universal distinction, that is a fair generalization of their approach in this kind of second group.

In his movement Beethoven does not set out to cause a conflict within the second group through the abrupt intervention of a contrasting statement, as does Mozart at m.24. The reason is the conflict Beethoven formerly introduced in mm.32-47, which is aggravated by two features: one is its sharply contrasted textural and thematic elements; the other is its successive tonal standpoints of A-flat major, F minor and D-flat major, all of which occur rapidly and are not strictly necessary in the tonal scheme of a transition. After that any further conflict might have proved destructive. Beethoven was alert enough to realize that a cumulative second group was needed. Mozart grants his second group key its tonal superiority through the use of a textural/thematic conflict, the inevitable approach where the second group key is not disturbed and the expository transition does not modulate.

If there is a model of *Shape ii* it is in the first movement of Mozart's *Symphony in G minor K.550*. It begins with a statement in two four-measure phrases, mm.44-47 and 48-51.

---

[8]Mm.87 and 89: This diminished seventh chord is theoretically not part of the key, since it is not on the primary, secondary or tertiary leading notes. It is harmonically a set of auxilliary notes (m.87) or passing notes (m.89).

The key is B-flat major. Its distinguishing feature is the descending chromatic scale. These two phrases are repeated from m.52 with new texture and with subtle modification of the harmony in mm.56-57. From the fourth quarter note of m.56 Mozart gives a row of 'dominant sevenths' by flattening the major third of each chord to become the flat seventh of the next; these are in the two violin parts alternately beginning with the F# in the first violin. This is nothing more than heavy key inflection and could have been used in mm.48-49 without damaging the cadence. But Mozart decided to defer its full effect until mm.56-57. There it almost compels the move to the 'dominant seventh of A-flat' in m.58.

What occurs in m.58 interrupts the repeated statement and introduces an extraordinary tonal standpoint. Here is new matter that harmonically amounts to a 'dominant seventh of A-flat in root position' alternating with a 'second inversion chord of A-flat major' for four measures (58-61). Thematically this is the simplest material and the texture, though still *piano*, is more densely orchestrated than the preceding statement. In juxtaposing the ambiguously related flat-seventh major tonal standpoint (A-flat major) against the second principal key (B-flat major) Mozart has created one of the worst possible tonal conflicts.

The way out is simplicity itself. First, he returns to the dominant seventh chord and begins a *crescendo* (m.62). He then moves the bass up one step from E-flat to E-natural, which makes a diminished seventh that is one of the secondary dominant chords of B-flat major. This enables him to proceed to the perfect cadence at m.66. The rising chromatic scale of mm.66-67 has a certain counterbalancing effect to the previous falling one, and it leads to another B-flat major cadence to give further resolution to this extraordinary conflict.[9]

It is interesting to note that through mm.72-88 the principal melodic figure of the first statement of the movement is prominent, and that there is a momentary inflection of B-flat major towards G minor – the key with which it was first associated. The principal purpose of this is to add just another skerrick of conflict to sustain the endorsement of the key of B-flat major through mm.72-99, all of which is very distinctly termination matter.

---

[9]It is hard to resist the temptation to describe this type of conflict/resolution as the 'rising Phoenix effect.' It is fairly common from the mid-1780s onwards, and this is undoubtedly one of the best examples. It is worth emphasizing too that in mm.58-66 Mozart is manipulating a tonal standpoint, and the rules or conventions of orthodox modulation do not apply.

Example III:14

row of domt.7ths $V^7 \quad - I^6_4$
See. Ex IV:7   of A♭ major

vii^0_7 /V
└─B♭ major

re-emerges →

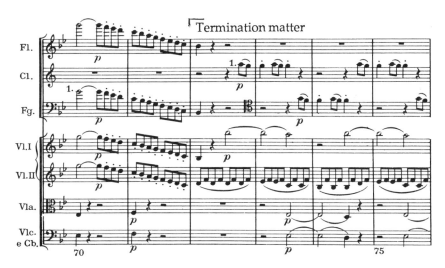

This particular second group is a very sophisticated one, whose key is challenged from the most remote tonal standpoint. In movements around the 1760s composers did no more than simply turn the second statement of the group into the minor mode,[10] then returned to the major for the remainder of the group. At the other extreme, some of the

[10]Second group keys are basically major, with the relatively few exceptions that are in the dominant minor from a minor tonic and a few others.

longer second groups of Beethoven's time have more than one point of significant conflict, each one having its own character and structural devices.

It seems to have been a practice of the 1790s that, where there was little or no tonal conflict in the first group and transition (including modulating transitions), the second group would adopt *Shape iii*. In the first movement of Beethoven's *Pianoforte Sonata in F op.2 no.1* the second group begins in the orthodox key of A-flat major in m.20 with a thrice stated falling dominant minor ninth arpeggio (Eb, G, Bb, Db, Fb) over an E-flat pedal.

Example III:15

This is, in fact, a reasonably serious state of conflict, even though it is in A-flat major. Its resolution is allowed to emerge only slowly, and it is not complete until m.41. After that Beethoven adds the termination mm.41-48. This is another of Beethoven's cumulative second groups.

A more usual course with *Shape iii* is to begin on a different tonal standpoint; the minor mode of the group's key is the preferred one. There are others, such as the relative minor (VI) of the tonic key. The first movement of Beethoven's *Pianoforte Sonata in C minor op.13* contains an example of the former. An expository transition occupies mm.25-40. The second group begins on cue at m.41 on E-flat minor.

Example III:16

32 = diminished 7th as secondary dominant of Eb minor

Getting to the orthodox key of E-flat major, which he does at m.79, is not simply a case of sharpening the third of the minor key. If E-flat major is to assume tonal superiority in place of the tonic, it must make an absolutely convincing entrance. To do that, it must resolve a preceding conflict and must not be upstaged by any other key or tonal standpoint. In *Shape iii* the composer must begin only with a tonal standpoint, so that the tonality remains relatively unstable.

The E-flat minor in the above example occurs only over its dominant pedal, mm.41-52. It is only a tonal standpoint. After repeating mm.41-44 as 49-52, mm.44-48 followed by mm.41-48 are then played on the dominant pedal of D-flat major as mm.53-64 . After touching E-flat minor once again (mm.65-69), F minor (mm.69-73) and with a very slight inflection to C minor (m.75), the chord progression carefully prepares for E-flat major at m.79. All this is based on the thematic element of mm.41-49. In other examples the composer may resort to two or three contrasting thematic elements treated separately and with a tonal structure that might be more diverse. But the principle behind each one amounts to what is outlined above.

In the new statement matter that follows the appearance of E-flat major at m.79, there are points of tonal inflection that spice the progressions sufficiently to justify the emphases of the cadences.

One aspect of some examples of *Shape iii* is the use of statement matter from the first group or transition late in the group. Here Beethoven recalls part of the first statement in mm.111-115, which are in the middle of the termination matter, mm.103-122.

Exercise 18

Examine and compare an example of a second group in each of the shapes described above. It will be necessary to relate each one to the first group and transition and to attempt to explain why the composer adopts particular features that occur.

The second group always ends with some kind of termination matter. This has been partly described above [p. 32ff]. Any assumption that the larger the exposition the longer is the termination proves false. That in the first movement of Beethoven's *Eroica* Symphony is a mere five measures, mm.144-148:

Example III:17

whereas in the first movement of his *Pianoforte Sonata in C minor op.13* it is twenty measures long, mm.103-122 (see *Example III:16*). The two examples are inevitably quite different in character.

Exercise 19

Examine a number of examples of termination occurring at the end of the exposition. Comment on their construction and on any thematic derivation. Assess the effectiveness of their function.

As was observed above, the character of the statement matter of the second group depends partly on the tonal structure of the group and partly on what happened in the preceding transition, and sometimes the first group as well. Therefore, each example has to be examined, described and judged for what it contains and how that is put to use throughout a movement. Haydn is one composer whose work has suffered badly from superficial and misguided commentary. Many have noticed his propensity for using the same thematic element at the beginning of the first group, the transition and the second group, and have jumped unwisely into expressions like 'monothematic works' and 'monothematic form.' One thing has to be understood about all diatonic music: *none* of it is 'monothematic' (based on one theme). When the term 'theme' is fully understood, it will be realized that the micro-structuring of the thematic elements is so diverse – arising from the need to relate new and old matter – that nothing monothematic has ever been written, and probably could not be.

In those cases where Haydn does re-use thematic elements, it will be found that a) quite new musical matter is composed; b) the new matter takes on a character related to its function in the total structure; and c) Haydn always includes some musical matter based on one or more different thematic elements.

Exercise 20

Examine the exposition of Haydn's *String Quartet in C major Hob.III.77*. Pay particular attention to the transformations of the Violin I figures of mm.1 and 2, the function of each transformation, and also the role of any new matter. Having done this compare it with the exposition of his *Symphony in G major Hob.I:94*.

Exercise 21

Examine the exposition of Beethoven's *Pianoforte Sonata in F minor op.57* (mm.1-65). Beware not to fall into the trap of pin-pointing m.35 as the start of the second group. Explain why it isn't.

4

Development

A consequence of the 'psychological step up' of the second group is that the emotional impetus of the music is increased. The development section must increase it still further, because in a large-scale movement this is far too early a point to decrease it.

The 'psychological step further up' is achieved through the deft combination of development, statement, transition and preparation matter, important to all of which is the progress of the tonality. Unlike the exposition, where there is a certain predictability about what may happen, there is no such predictability about the development section; save that in its final stages, it will prepare in some way for the return of the tonic key and for the recapitulation. What types of matter it uses at different points, what exposition matter is drawn on and to what extent it is modified, what new matter is introduced, and what the progression of keys and tonal standpoints is etc., are entirely at the composer's discretion. Therefore, for each development section the composer must devise a particular strategy, at the root of which will be an appropriate pattern of resolved conflicts.

The second principal key establishes its tonal superiority with the second group. The composer's first task in the development section is to break that key's hold, and sometimes that is done in conjunction with preparing the return to the tonic for the repeat of the exposition. There are different approaches to the problem; here, they are recognized as six different approaches.

i. Those that begin with the second group key and continue with development matter.

   Examples: Haydn, *String Quartet in C major Hob.III:77*
   Beethoven, *Pianoforte Sonata in A major op.101*

ii. Those that begin with a tonal standpoint other than those found in the exposition, and continue with development matter.

   Examples: Mozart, *Pianoforte Sonata in C major K.279*

Beethoven, *Pianoforte Sonata in D minor op.31 no.2*

iii. Those that continue after a clean break with the second group key and then move through transition matter to a new key for the introduction of either new or old matter, which might be statement or development.

Examples: Haydn, *String Quartet in F major Hob.III:82*
Beethoven, *Pianoforte Sonata in F minor op.2 no.1*

iv. Those that are like iii., but begin with a sudden change of key.

Examples: Beethoven, Pianoforte Sonatas *op.2 no.3, op.7* and *op.10 no.1.*

v. Those that have a modulatory or transition passage closely linking the end of the exposition with the development section proper. An interesting example occurs in the first movement of Beethoven's *Pianoforte Sonata in C major op.53*

Example IV:1

A climactic E major cadence is reached at m.74. Whether this marks the end of the second group is highly debatable; certainly it is unusual to have this kind of climactic trill in or at the end of that section. While mm.74ff sound and function like termination matter, they are first inflected to A minor, then turned fully into E minor. The passage is repeated an octave lower, mm.78-82. This allows

Beethoven to reach C major at m.86a for the repeat of the exposition, or to go on through m.86b to the development proper, which begins on F major in m.90 with a shortened version of the first statement. It was Beethoven who, with this kind of transition matter, gradually devised close dovetailing of the principal sections of a sonata form movement.

vi. Those that begin with a complete statement of entirely new matter in the key of the second group. Mozart had a fondness for this. For example, in the first movement of his *Pianoforte Sonata in F major K.332* he has two very clean-cut eight-measure phrases, which are repeated an octave lower before the section goes on with development matter.

Example IV:2

The development section of his *Pianoforte Sonata in G major K.283* (see Example IV:3 below) comprises only a nine-measure statement of entirely new matter which is followed by a dominant preparation of the tonic, also based on entirely new matter. This, however, is an exceptional case.

Since the development section is less than predictable in its content and structure, only discussion of individual examples can convey the full extent of that. Some restriction has to be placed here on a topic that could, itself, take up all of a substantial book. Therefore, the next part of this chapter is devoted to four specific and instructive examples.

Example IV:3

Exercise 22

Before continuing with this chapter, re-examine carefully the expositions of the first movements of the following works:

i. Beethoven, *Pianoforte Sonata in C minor op.10 no.1*

ii. Haydn, *String Quartet in C major Hob.III:77*

iii. Beethoven, *Pianoforte Sonata in C major op.53*

iv. Mozart, *Symphony in G minor K.550*

i. Beethoven, Pianoforte Sonata in C minor op.10 no.1

The exposition ends in m.105 in the conventional key of E-flat major (see *Example III:13*). The two quarter rests following the single quarter-note chord make a clean break between either the repeat of the exposition or the development section. The former begins with a *forte* C minor chord, the latter with a *forte* C major chord.

There is a similarity between the opening measures and mm.106-114; the *piano* figure is now higher in pitch, and it seems Beethoven deliberately intended that the first quarter note of mm.110 and 114 be *piano*, not *forte* as in m.5. This is, however, a transition, in which C major is only the initial tonal standpoint. Maintaining the same texture as mm. 108-110, the leading note diminished seventh chord (omitting its root, B-natural) of mm.112-113 moves to a diminished seventh on E-natural. Thus, instead of being forced into the new matter of m.9, Beethoven grants himself open-ended harmony to use the second figure again as dominant harmony to F (not yet defined as major or minor) through

Example IV:4

mm.114-117. With it he harks back to the right hand leaps of mm.28-30. The diminished seventh of mm.112-113 functions as the secondary dominant of F.

The m.1 matter has now been well-used, and the dominant preparation precludes its further use here. Beethoven has to find something new to the context. His choice is either to adapt something from the other exposition matter or to compose something new. Whatever it was, it must begin like a strong statement; development matter would not be suitable. There are three items of statement matter in the exposition that Beethoven might consider; namely, those in mm.9, 32 and 56. The first is not at all suitable, because it is 'appendage' matter rather than a 'starter,' and it can be compared with the descending chromatic scale in Mozart's *Pianoforte Sonata in C minor K.457 (Example III:1)* The second lacks the sense of urgency needed, mainly because of its texture and its short-breathed phrase, which would have needed considerable adaption to turn it into a suitable statement. Further, its juxtaposition against the right hand leaps has already occurred and for it to do so again would be re-hashing the exposition as the development, a procedure that would mitigate against its function. The strong reason for not using the third, m.56 matter, is again the short-breathed phrase. A further reason is that it lacks a suitable figure for continuity in development; this one has rather too wide a compass.

Beethoven took the obvious course of writing a new and more suitable statement. Yet it is interesting to note the similarity of its texture to that of mm.56ff, and some parallels between its melodic outline and those of mm.33ff and 56ff, though it is not derived from either. It is an eight-measure statement in F minor (mm.118-125), which is repeated with a slightly varied left hand and *crescendo/diminuendo* in B-flat minor. To this is added the last figure moved up to D-flat major (mm.133-136).

This single-process development section has been dominated so far by transition and statement matter. From m.136 it introduces development matter. First are six measures of *Figure A*, which is taken from mm.120-121, in D-flat major turning through mm.140-141 to B-flat minor, where new matter occurs. The right hand of m.142ff has a vague resemblance to that of mm.33ff. They are different from the preceding six measures, but keep up their momentum with left hand quarter notes. It forms a four-measure figure that moves to F minor, then is repeated to move to C minor with the two right hand parts inverted. The sequence is next shortened to lead to the *fortissimo* climax at m.154, which in turn leads to the dominant preparation at m.158 via the secondary dominant (a diminished seventh) on the last quarter note of m.157. It is to be noted that the secondary dominant is not used prior to m.157, so the appearance of C minor in m.150 is not secure. The preparation is the harmonized falling scale of C harmonic minor. It is repeated and leads directly into the recapitulation.

Exercise 23

Compare the development sections of the first movements of Beethoven's *Pianoforte Sonata in C minor op.10 no.1* and Mozart's *Pianoforte Sonata in C minor K.457*.

ii. Haydn, String Quartet in C major Hob.III:77

This is a rather different example of a development section from the previous one. It occupies mm.44b-78 and can be divided into two contrasting processes at m.64. The musical matter of the first process is entirely development and its texture, theme and tonality change rapidly throughout, as Haydn moves from one developed fragment to another. Here he demonstrates complete mastery of micro-level conflict, which, had it been used with poor technique and to excess, would have brought the listener to total confusion. At the right moment

Example IV:5

he works towards an E minor tonal standpoint and brings about some stability through a two-measure phrase (mm.60-61), which is repeated *piano* and then extended (mm.62-64) and proves to be a preparation.

The second process begins on the *forte* of m.64 in total contrast to anything heard so far. Haydn's fondness for the folk music of his native Lower Austria shows itself in this passage, with its alternating *sforzando* open fifths in the 'cello and viola. The key is E major for what is a well-formed statement. The first measure draws on the m.1 violin figure. That immediately gives way to new melodic figures in mm.65-67, which recur during the course of the statement. The dotted rhythm melody of mm.68ff can be attributed in part to mm.8-12, though the derivation is by no means direct. The phrase that embraces it is repeated and extended by one measure (m.74).

Next, using two of these figures in a two-measure phrase, now E-minor and *piano*, repeated *pianissimo*, Haydn prepares for something. This is not a preparation based on the dominant harmony of the subsequent key, but it is none the less preparation. After the instability of the first process and the forcefulness of the second up to m.74, then poising as Haydn does on the E minor standpoint from m.75, repeating the phrase so quietly, and finally adding the four quarter beats of graced E to an E minor chord through m.78, he creates an intolerable conflict. It is only satisfactorily resolved by the sudden *forte* switch to C major for the recapitulation.

iii. Beethoven, Pianoforte Sonata in C major op.53

The link between the end of the second group and either the repeat of the exposition or the start of the development section proper has been described above (pp.90-91). Like the previous example, this one has two distinct development processes; yet it is very different. At m.90 Beethoven introduces a shortened version of the B-flat portion of the first statement on F major; E in the bass in m.92 is flattened in m.93, as was A in mm.7-8. [see *Example II:2*] Just as m.9 moved to the dominant of C minor, so m.94 moves to the dominant of G minor. There the parallel ends, because Beethoven now composes development matter based on the melodic figures of m.3 and m.4. These figures are shortened in mm.96ff and there joined in the left hand by the sixteenth notes drawn from m.14ff. G minor survives until m.99, where C minor is juxtaposed and mm.96-99 are repeated, though with less pitch distance between the two melodic figures. The dynamics of the G minor and C minor measures are the same; Beethoven does not actually specify *piano* at m.96. On F minor at a much higher pitch and *pianissimo* Beethoven composes a new phrase based on the first melodic figure of the preceding phrase (m.104). Beethoven's reason for this is to slide quickly using a falling sequence through the remote tonal standpoints of C-flat major (m.105), B-flat minor (m.106), A-flat major (m.107), G-flat major (m.108) back to F minor at m.109. C-flat major, A-flat major and F minor are the more prominent. A *crescendo* leads via the Italian sixth secondary dominant at the end of m.111 to the dominant of F and the next process at m.112.

Example IV:6

A useful device of development and one that undermines any sense of key or tonal standpoint is successive dominant or diminished sevenths. In the following chord progression, it will be seen that a series of major chords each has the minor seventh added by flattening the third (equivalent to the leading note) of the previous chord.

Example IV:7

In the invention of development matter the composer may use this progression on any scale from as little as quarter notes to two or even more measures. It may be elaborated by extending these chords to the minor ninth or placing other chords between them, while still retaining them as the focal points of the progression.

Drawing on the matter from m.50 of the exposition Beethoven begins the second process on the dominant of F, using only the chord C-E-G. This becomes the minor ninth, C-E-G-B♭-D♭, in mm.114-115.[1] These four measures are repeated as mm.116-119, F major to B-flat major; then again mm.120-123, B-flat major to E-flat, but now minor. Three times is enough for any sequence, and Beethoven wisely turned away from it. The chord progression from m.124 is:

- 124-125:   E-flat minor
- 126-127:   an enharmonic F-sharp (for G-flat) major to the seventh[2]
- 128-129:   B (for C-flat) minor
- 130-131:   G major to the seventh
- 132-133:   C minor
- 134:   D-flat major
- 135:   Diminished seventh on F-sharp

---

[1]The second half of m.112 is the secondary dominant of F major. The strange point in the passage is the second half of m.113, where Beethoven clashes the secondary dominant (the diminished seventh, B-D-A♭) in the right hand against an F minor chord in the left. Since Beethoven clearly intended mm.112-115 to be the dominant of F major (the secondary dominant of m.112 and the F major chord of mm.116 are the proof), the Cs of the ninth and twelfth eighth notes of the left hand can only be explained by regarding them as part of a pedal C through the harmony. That Beethoven did this deliberately is clear from the autograph and its parallels in mm.117 and 121. Theoretically it is incorrect.

[2]The progression through mm.126-133 can be compared with mm.266-272 of the first movement of Beethoven's *Pianoforte Sonata in B-flat major op.106*, where, contrary to the assertions of some, the tonal standpoint of m.267 is not B minor. It is C-flat minor, a key that no sensible composer would attempt to notate.

- 136-140:   G major to the seventh with C minor and D major to the seventh included over the pedal G.
- 140-141:   a chord progression in C minor leading to the preparation of 142-155.

This extraordinary chord progression, which mocks the terms key and tonal standpoint, is another illustration of the extent to which the later sonata composers were able and prepared to go in pursuit of the principle this book hopes to make clear. Beethoven begins to emerge from the deepest point of the conflict as he comes close to the C minor tonality of mm.132ff. He uses the neapolitan chord in m.134 to add firmness, as it always does to an approach to the tonic. Having maintained the *forte* to m.136 and clearly intending the tide of emotion to subside gradually, Beethoven sinks to *piano* (the *forte* in m.138 is a last gasp), then descends further to *pianissimo* and the dominant chord of the tonic, C major (m.142).

In most development sections the deepest point of conflict is held back as long as possible so that the emotional impetus can be kept continuous into the recapitulation. Here Beethoven appears to abandon the convention. At the same time he presents himself with the problem of how to cut into the recapitulation. In fact, what he does show is that the preparation of m.142 does not mark a point of resolution, but still one of intense conflict. The moment he strikes the first beat the music is propelled forward; it would be a mistake to conclude that Beethoven had to force it. It went entirely of its own accord and any attempt to obstruct it would have been disastrous.

This is an unusual preparation and its length has been commented on. Yet relative to the length of the movement, (302 measures), these fourteen measures are not out of proportion. Other preparations are actually and relatively longer. This one is notable because it starts *pianissimo* and builds gradually to a *fortissimo* with ever-increasing movement, such that an intense climax at the extremes of the compass is reached at m.154. It must collapse, and does so through the contrary motion scales of m.155 into the first statement *pianissimo* and the recapitulation. The length and characteristic of this preparation is determined not so much by what has gone before, but by what follows it. A recapitulation that begins *piano* or *pianissimo*, and few do, usually has a *forte* or *fortissimo* immediately preceding it. Beethoven had to prepare the m.155 *fortissimo* thoroughly, and doing so – from a *pianissimo* through these fourteen measures – was another of his master strokes.

iv. Mozart, *Symphony in G minor, K.550*

The exposition ends in m.99. The chord in m.100 is the dominant seventh of G minor in second inversion, and the next in m.101 (and m.1) is G minor in root position.

Example IV:8

The stepwise descending bass is important to the progression here, because it leads to the second chord of m.101 – a diminished seventh on the sharpened tonic (i.e., G#, the tertiary leading note) of G minor. This is the point from which Mozart would move to a new tonal centre. Before he discloses his intention, he picks out from the chord B-natural and D and gives them to the woodwind as a *piano* whole note. There are four tonal centres to which he could have moved directly from this diminished seventh chord: A, C, E-flat and F-sharp/G-flat. Only as the woodwind falling thirds and the violin figure of the first statement emerge does one sense that it is to be F-sharp minor.[3] The sudden switching of the tonality from B-flat major, through G minor to the edge of the unknown is excellent conflict creation. By m.102 the mind is very puzzled. Only by holding that measure for a whole note, then as the thirds fall, gently allowing the first violin figure to emerge from the mist, does Mozart make a satisfactory resolution. It is worth noting too that Mozart treats the first violin figure as an anacrusis to m.105, much as he had done in mm.20-21, and in contrast to the opening of the movement.

Consider now mm.105-114, which begin like a statement, but soon prove to be another piece of devastating conflict through transition matter. The very morale and vigor of the music are sapped as it wilts inexorably. Causing the music to wilt is another approach to conflict creation; and, naturally, there is a consequently different approach to its resolution. With perfect timing and complete surprise, Mozart arrests the wilting with a *forte* development passage in two-part counterpoint in the strings (violins against violas and 'cellos) with some woodwind

---

[3]Or in the complex world of enharmonic notation this might just be G-flat minor, a key that exists in theory, but which in the equal-tempered system is too cumbersome to notate.

harmonization (m.114ff).[4] At m.118 he inverts the two string parts and sequences the phrase, inverting it and sequencing it again at mm.122 and 126. The tonal standpoints are E minor (m.114), A minor (m.118), D minor (m.120), continuing by falling fifths every two measures to B-flat major at m.128. The phrase that would have ended in m.130, prior to another inversion is instead extended by a sequence of the previous two bars a tone lower, and again another tone lower until it arrives on the dominant of D minor at m.134. The conflict of mm.114-128 and the thrice stated sequence of mm.128-134 force Mozart to provide some respite, and he does so through holding the dominant of D minor through mm.134-138 as a preparation.

It would have been easy for Mozart to dovetail these measures into a full statement of the first group; but that would have been absurd. The key is the dominant, the first time it has enjoyed any prominence. What must not happen here is the appearance of the first group in the dominant, because it would either upstage its return in the tonic for the recapitulation, or cause the postponement of the recapitulation for so long that an inordinately long development section would ensue. Mozart was too wise to fall into that trap. Yet he put the tonality into the wrong position and had to take care that the tonic key was not upstaged and made to sound too much like the subdominant in relationship to this point. He gets out of his deliberately arranged difficulty by resorting to the now familiar device: creating another and even deeper conflict and resolving it into what is required.

G minor   C major   125   F major

---

[4]The last part of the development section of the previous example (Beethoven's *Opus 53*) might be viewed in this light. The arrest of that wilting occurs with the start of the preparation.

Bb major
Preparation

Development matter

130

Dominant of D minor

135

Bb minor
D minor aborted

At m.138 the texture is suddenly thinned out and the dynamic level taken down to *piano*. Far from resolving the previous conflict, this only makes it worse. Added to that is the extraordinary juxtaposed tonal standpoint of B-flat minor through mm.139-142, followed by C minor in mm.142-146. Neither has anything to do with D minor or each other, and it is only through the thinness of the texture that Mozart gets away with blue murder. Nevertheless, at m.146 he has what he needs: a diminished seventh on F-sharp, despite the fact that it will take him some time to turn that into a secure dominant preparation of G minor.

To take the conflict still deeper, he causes that diminished seventh to wilt through mm.146-152 by having it fall in three steps in the strings, each punctuated by the woodwind, but with this figure adding the disturbing new feature of accented dissonance. While the diminished seventh chord is a discord, the first note of the rhythm in the first violin and 'cello parts are not part of it. The second violins and violas articulate on the fourth and second quarter notes; and that is where the first violins and 'cellos must also put their accents, unlike all other uses of this figure, where they must be on the first and third quarter notes. Performance that way only intensifies the conflict.

By m.152 the whole situation has become intolerable. Mozart must arrest it and rid himself of it. Over a pedal D in the horns he begins the dominant preparation with a measure-length progression of V^9 - I - vii $^0_7$/V - V^7 - I,   followed by three chords in mm.158-159 in rapid succession accenting the tertiary, primary and secondary dominants in that order. Finally he settles on to a quiet decline into the recapitulation.

1 = primary dominant
2 = secondary dominant ⎤ in G minor
3 = tertiary dominant ⎦

Again, Mozart does not resort to immediate resolution of the conflict of mm.138-152. Instead, through arresting the wilting of mm.146-152 with a new *forte* texture and alternating the figure between upper strings and the tutti basses against a new figure in the woodwind, he deepens it still further. In mm.160-166 the music merely poises until the first statement can be dovetailed in, in the same way that it was in mm.20-21 and 103-105.

165

⌊G minor

The four examples described above are progressively more difficult to grasp; but when associated with a study of examples of similar proportions, these different approaches to the composition of the development section should convey some understanding of the possibilities. The limitation of space here is sufficient to resolve any conflict in the temptation to describe all those other examples that contain fascinating features and pose intriguing questions. There are, however, two matters that are worth clearing up. One concerns the common but misleading term *retransition*; the other is the so-called *false reprise* of Haydn.

The term *retransition* is often used to describe the approach to the recapitulation. What has to be determined is what type of musical matter is found in that place. Immediately before the recapitulation there is invariably some form of preparation, and immediately before that is either development matter or statement – though only rarely the latter. What is not found is transition matter. Therefore, this misleading term is one that is better dispensed with.

Haydn has been credited with writing in some of his works a *false reprise* or *premature reprise*; that is, he is said to have written a return to the first statement in the tonic key within the development section. This is arrant nonsense. With the few exceptions described at the beginning of the next chapter, the recapitulation occurs where the tonic key is re-established and associated with the first statement of the movement. Some of Haydn's recapitulations are unusually structured; but viewed in the light of the idea of this book, they are clear and explicable. Haydn never wrote a 'false' or 'premature' reprise within the development section (neither did any other competant composer) because the one key that *must not* and *does not* assume any prominence within the development section is the tonic key.

Exercise 24

Examine one or two examples of the occurrence of new matter in the development section. Consider how this new matter is prepared, and distinguish between those examples that could be classified as statement and those that could not. Both Mozart's and Beethoven's pianoforte sonatas contain interesting examples. A notable one requiring some thought and preparatory work is in the first movement of Beethoven's *Eroica* symphony.

5

Recapitulation
and Coda

A: Recapitulation

The function of the recapitulation and coda is to resolve the macro-conflicts of the movement, so that it can be finished off. That is sometimes done by repeating all or most of the statement matter of the exposition in the tonic key, and then adding sufficient termination matter to make the conclusion convincing. However, this is a very simplistic view of what is often a difficult section of the movement to compose. Mere repetition of a large tract of previously heard musical matter in one key may result in boredom at a point where the interest of the listener must be kept alive to the last. Therefore, the recapitulation and coda must have carefully contrived conflicts, which may be entirely new or variants of previous ones. Some of them are inevitable. Others arise from the composer's judgement of the total plan of the movement and of the last part in particular. Most of them occur around the end of the first group, during the transition and at the beginning of the coda; some occur within the first and second groups. They can rely entirely on the textural and thematic elements, but principally they resort to tonal conflict. In other words, the obliging composer puts some gin in the tonic.

The vast majority of recapitulations begin with the first statement of the movement in the tonic key, though often with varied, sometimes radically varied texture. There is sound reason for this. The start of the recapitulation is the first point of macro-conflict resolution. The deeper the preceding conflicts, the more secure that point must be. Since the listener's clearest recollection is most likely to be the firm, assertive and neatly designed first statement, its occurrence, here, in association with the tonic key is the most likely way to provide the greatest degree of primary resolution.[1] There is a secondary reason for this: in view of the modifications that must be made immediately after it, in order to retain the tonic key for the second group, a very high degree of stability is required at the start of the recapitulation.

What of examples that do not begin in this way? That is: 1) those that do not begin with the thematic element of the first statement; 2) those that do not begin in the tonic key, but revert to it quickly; and 3) those that repeat the exposition more-or-less note-for-note beginning in the subdominant and ending inevitably in the tonic. As there are relatively few examples of these, and since they are abnormal, each must be examined and interpreted for what it is. There are extremes. The first movement of Schubert's *Pianoforte Quintet in A major op.114 'The Trout'* is a well-known example of the third type. None could deny the beguiling nature of its tunes; but, and without apology for any heresy, it is a structural disaster, one of the reasons for which is the subdominant recapitulation. On the other hand, in his *Pianoforte Sonata in F major op.10 no.2* Beethoven begins the first movement's recapitulation in the extraordinary key of D major. This is not a question of academic right or wrong, but an artist's judgement of a particular set of circumstances. This strange manoeuvre can be justified when viewed in the light of the exposition's first group and transition (which does not appear in this recapitulation) and the second group of both the exposition and recapitulation.

Exercise 25

Find and list for later study some examples of recapitulations that fall into each of the three categories given above. Exclude Haydn's music from this search.

Where an exposition has used a modulatory transition, the composer must make a structural modification for the recapitulation – the third of the types described above excepted. One way is to modify the previous transition, another is to write an entirely new one, another is to omit the transition altogether and juxtapose the first and second groups. Yet another is to modify the end of the first group or beginning of the second group, or both, possibly in conjuction with some restructuring of the transition. What the composer decides to do in this area, and in other areas of the recapitulation, depends entirely on what is made inevitable by the exposition's structure and what arises from the composer's own strategy; and in turn, these depend on the scale the composer has chosen for the movement.

Three examples are discussed. In each one the problem of how to retain the tonic key while maintaining the continuity of the movement is solved in a different way.

---

[1]That is, of course, a subsidiary reason for having that kind of statement at the beginning of the movement.

Exercise 26

Re-examine the expositions and development sections of the first movements of the following works before proceeding to the commentaries which follow.

Beethoven, *Pianoforte Sonata in E major op.14 no.1*
Mozart, *Symphony in G minor K.550*
Beethoven, *Pianoforte Sonata in C major op.53*

i. Beethoven, *Pianoforte Sonata in E major op.14 no.1*

The recapitulation begins at m.91, preceded by a preparation derived from first statement matter. The preparation is in the minor, but turns to the major at m.90. The first statement is structurally the same, but with the texture of the first four measures radically changed. (see *Example I:16*) The right hand now plays chords, while the left hand plays rising sixteenth note scales. The dynamic of the first figure is now *forte*; it reverts to *piano* for the second figure. The second group is also the same, transposed to the tonic key. There is a minor amendment to m.135-136 because of the upper limit of f^3 of the pianoforte's compass when this work was written.[2]

Example V:1

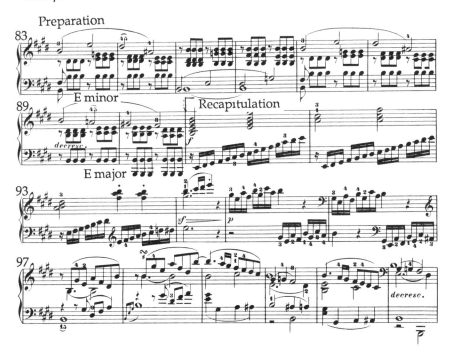

---

[2]He did write f#³ in m.41. It is considered a slip.

The transition occupies mm.103-113, compared with mm.13-22. Its preparation portion is structurally the same, though the notes are redistributed. The radical change is in the first portion. Beethoven could not resume the first statement's theme in m.103 in the tonic. The reason does not lie in the mere fact of using the tonic again at that point, but in the absence of some other significant tonal and even thematic conflict in the first and second groups.[3] The little he introduced through the revised texture of mm.91-94 is insufficient to sustain the movement to the end. Faced with a dull prospect Beethoven always takes the plunge. A *decrescendo* in m.102 yields a *pianissimo* chord on the flat sixth of E major, namely C major. This again is not a key, merely a tonal standpoint for three measures over a C-natural pedal. He retains the textural image of m.91 (rising scales below chords derived from the first statement), then makes a quick *crescendo* through m.105 to a German augmented sixth chord (C-E-G-A#) in m. 106. He treats the C major standpoint as being on the E minor side, the quick and sure way out which is via an augmented sixth chord on the pedal C. The diminished seventh (the secondary dominant) to dominant progression of mm.107-112 smooths over the previous *major tonic/flat-sixth major* conflict and E major returns secure and authoritative in m.113. By revising the texture of the first statement, then countering that with the dynamically contrasted flat sixth version of the same thematic element, Beethoven caused just enough conflict to sustain interest to the movement's end.

---

[3]The second group does have the slight tonal shift to F-sharp minor in m.115 and the alternating major/minor sixth through mm.137-140; both occur also in the exposition, but neither is a ddep conflict.

Exercise 27

Compare the recapitulation to the start of the second group of
the above example with the corresponding passage in the first
movement of Haydn's *Symphony in C major Hob.I:97*

ii. Mozart, *Symphony in G minor K.550*

    Example V:2

Vn & Va/Vc parts inverted

└─ F minor   200

Extension of F minor portion

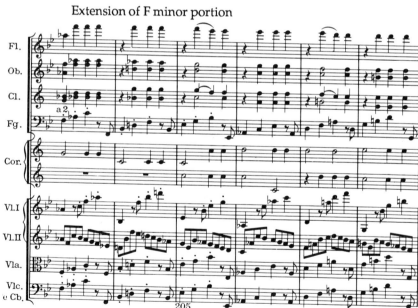

205

Structurally as mm.28-42 G minor

210

G minor

215   220

The first group of the recapitulation occupies mm.164-183. It is the same as mm.1-20, with the exception of its entrance and the added bassoon part in mm.168-172. The transition begins exactly as before, and it is here that Mozart ran the risk of having an excess of tonic. Fortunately, he had insured himself against that through the use of the expository matter in m.28. The principle of 'new key demands new theme' now turns itself around to that of 'new theme demands new key.' Mozart may keep the same thematic element; but if he does, he must find a new tonality for it. Since m.191 cannot be in B-flat major or the 'psychological step up' with the same manoeuvre would recur where it shouldn't, Mozart had to look for 'psychological step down' or at most 'psychological step sideways.' The four keys in which the m.28 matter could recur are E-flat major, F major, C minor and D minor. As both D minor and F major are on the sharp side and are effectively 'psychological step up,' the choice fell between E-flat major and C minor, the latter 'step down' and the former 'step sideways.' Mozart's choice was clear, and so mm.185-187 begin the move to E-flat major with appropriate modification of the thematic and tonal elements.

Since G minor, not E-flat major, is to be the key of the second group, Mozart must now get out of the position into which he has been forced to put himself. In progressing from m.191 E-flat must be regarded as the temporary tonic. Therefore, Mozart extends the phrase to modulate to F minor[4] at m. 198, where he inverts the treble and bass figuration and plays the m.28 matter again. He modifies and extends it even more through to m.211, where mm.28-42 occur as mm.211-225 almost as before, but in G minor. All is then ready for the proper entrance of the second group.

iii. Beethoven, *Pianoforte Sonata in C major op.53*

Example V:3

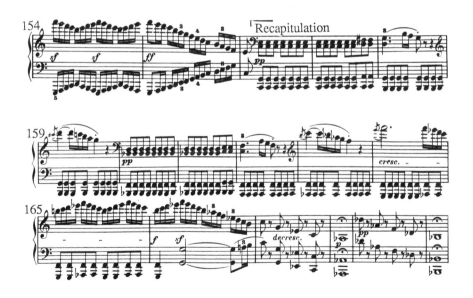

---

[4]that is, the supertonic relating back to E-flat major, not the key on the flat-seventh, F major, relating forward to G minor. There is no relationship between E-flat major and F major.

As with the Mozart movement above, the exposition's transition of this example also begins with the thematic element of the first statement in the tonic key then moves to new matter. The tonality at m.23 is E minor, so that the second group can be in the indirectly related key of E major. However, Beethoven's approach to the recapitulation transition and its continuation into the second group is a little different from Mozart's.

The recapitulation transition begins in m.174, as it did in m.14. Of course, it must not take the 'psychological step up' to E major. Like Mozart, who went to the subdominant side of B-flat major, Beethoven goes – adding one bar – to the subdominant side of the E minor of m.23, namely A minor at m.184. Instead of doing as Mozart did to get to the tonic key for the start of the second group, Beethoven merely continues with the transition exactly as before and thus begins the second group in A major. And the way out of that? After four measures m.200 switches to A minor; and without altering the structure of mm.39-41, Beethoven modulates to the required C major for the rest of the second group.

Beethoven avoids, even with the unusual start to the second group, deepening the conflict of this passage as much as Mozart had done. The reason lies a little further back. The first group was repeated exactly up to the last note (mm.156-167), where Beethoven makes an odd twist, the purpose of which is to prolong the existing conflict caused by the juxtaposition of the tonic and flat seventh tonalities. Instead of settling on an octave G at m.168, he substitutes A-flat. This prompts the sequence down the D-flat major chord, then the E-flat major chord, and finally an abrupt turn through the diminished seventh to a cadential progression in C major. Together with the amended transition through m.181-184 and the start of the second group, this provides quite enough conflict for this stage of the movement.

Exercise 28

Explain the transition of the recapitulation of the first movement of Beethoven's *Pianoforte Sonata in F minor op.57*. The clue lies in the juxtaposition of the major and minor modes.

In cases where there is a non-modulatory transition in the exposition, some examples retain in the recapitulation the unchanged first group and transition then continue with the second group in the tonic key. The first movement of Mozart's *Pianoforte Sonata in D major K.284* is typical of this type.

Example V:4

This kind of repetition with only the key of the second group changed is all that is required for a movement as light as this.[5] Beethoven, in contrast, had to take a different view of the non-modulatory transition. The exposition transition of the first movement of his *String Quartet in C minor op.18 no.4* [see *Example I:18*] occupies mm.13-25 and contains three

---

[5]Mozart does add one measure (m.97) to raise the pitch of the continuation, so that m.102 can be at the better compass.

thematic elements; namely, the *fortissimo* chords of mm.13-16, a slight recollection of the first group in mm.17-19, and the preparation of mm.20-25. In the recapitulation transition the second two are dispensed with and the chords extended from C minor to touch D-flat major and E-flat minor before settling back on to the dominant of C. This turns out to be major, so that the second group can retain the major mode.

Example V:5

Exercise 29

Compare the transitions of the exposition and recapitulation of the first movement of Beethoven's *Pianoforte Sonata in C major op.2 no.3*.

While, as was stated above, the vast majority of recapitulations begin with the first statement of the movement in the tonic key, there are a few notable exceptions. Three unusual types have been identified already [p. 114]; but there is one more. This is the one in which the first statement begins as before and in the tonic key; but without any delay, it is radically modified to introduce a conflict that the composer is hindered from providing elsewhere, but which it is vitally necessary to have somewhere. One such example is in the first movement of Beethoven's *Eroica* Symphony.

The framework of the second group remains the same in both the exposition (mm.45-148) and the recapitulation (mm.448-551). The transition (mm.37-45 and 440-448) is quite short and its structure only slightly modified at its end in the recapitulation. What precedes it in the exposition is a two-conflicts first group. These have their beginnings in mm.7 and 18 and both undermine the same thematic element. Comparing mm.398-439 with 3-36 one finds a radically new first group, the notable features of which are: 1) the juxtaposition of F major at m.408

Example V:6

Exp.

13

Recap.

406

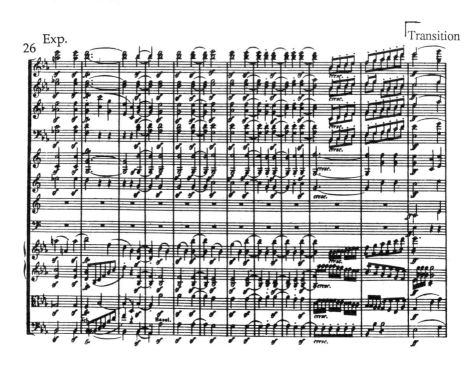

dominant of Eb

against the preceding E-flat major, thus overshadowing the conflict caused by the C# of m.7 in m.402; and then 2) the juxtaposition of D-flat major in m.416 against its preceding F major, and the dominant seventh of E-flat major against the D-flat major at m.424. The C-flat of the basses (m.423) is a hint of E-flat minor, which doesn't materialize. While there are thematic and tonal elements of the second part of the exposition's first group in mm.430-440, the result is quite different because of the telescoped rhythm and the removal of all the musical matter of mm.23-36.

Beethoven's reason for all this is clear. The short transition does not lend itself, without very radical alteration, to his predilection for a significant conflict in that area. There is enough in the second group already. The first group is ideal for his purpose, and his judgement about it could not be bettered.

As with most first groups, modifications to second groups are few, but they are all made for the selfsame reason: to deepen the conflict where required in order to keep the movement alive. Where the modification occurs depends entirely on the particular circumstances of the movement and the group.

Exercise 30

Compare the recapitulations of the first movements of Beethoven's *Pianoforte Sonata in C minor op.10 no.1* and his *Pianoforte Sonata in C minor op.13*.

Where the mode is changed from the related major key in the exposition to the minor tonic in the recapitulation, some modification of the second group becomes unavoidable.[6] An obvious case is the first movement of Mozart's *Symphony in G minor K.550*. The exposition's second group has been described above [pp. 75-81]. In the recapitulation the key is changed from B-flat major to G minor, which forces Mozart into some significant re-harmonization. His first problem is in m.46 (repeated in m.54), where he used the chord II_5^6 as the secondary dominant. This chord cannot be used in the minor, because it confuses the mode.[7] Thus, m.229 is substantially, and cleverly, re-harmonized. The viola and bass parts are given contrary moving chromatic scales, so that the last quarter note is theoretically a French augmented sixth (Eb-G-A-C#), one of the minor key's secondary dominants, though due to the tempo it is hardly heard as that.

Example V:7

VI V_5^6/V I_4^6 I

* C major inflexion
ϕ French Aug. 6th

Mozart's next problem is the falling chromatic scale of mm.48-49 (and 56-57), where it begins on the major sixth above the key-note, and mm.231-232 (and 239-240) where it begins on the minor sixth above the key-note. In the exposition the falling scale ends on the dominant seventh of the flat-seventh major (A-flat). Were Mozart to have placed the flat-seventh major chord in m.241, this would have been the result:

---

[6]Some are reprised in the major without alteration; the minor might be resumed for the coda.

[7]See the footnote on p. 64.

Example V:8

The repeated B-flat is melodically unsatisfactory and the chord progression across the second and third measures even less so. Now, were Mozart to have permitted the treble part to fall one more semitone, he would have produced a totally unacceptable position from which to make a return to G minor, quite apart from the hideous nature of the chord progression across the second and third measures:

Example V:9

Mozart decides to allow the treble part to fall a whole tone to A-flat for the dominant seventh of E-flat major, itself a close relative of G minor, as was evident at m.191 in the transition. The return to G minor from the flat-sixth rather than the flat-seventh calls for further modification; therefore, the five entirely new measures, mm.247-251, are inserted to make the restoration of G minor quite secure.

Example V:10

V⁷ – I₄⁶ of E♭ major

Five measures inserted to restore G minor

G minor

With two modifications the rest of the second group is structurally the same. One is replacing the inflection of G minor at m.265 and m.273 with C minor instead of E-flat major (cf. m.77 and 85; and see   p. 76. The other is the enlargement of the exposition's termination (mm.88-99) with the insertion of mm.280-292 in place of those corresponding to mm.92-94.

As a result of transposing the exposition's second group into the tonic key for the recapitulation, the question of whether the transposition should be up or down inevitably arises. This is purely a matter of the role the texture plays in achieving the effects the composer wants. What occurs at any point must be considered in the light of what goes before and after, and what modifications are being made to the thematic and tonal elements of the exposition's matter. *Example V:4* is one where Mozart adds one measure to the previous second group to obtain the better position in the compass.

Exercise 31

Compare and comment on some examples containing significant changes of texture in the recapitulation. Note especially those that arise from the transposition of the second group.

Haydn's recapitulations have been commented on frequently for failing to repeat the musical matter of the exposition in the same order, as Mozart and Beethoven did, and in fact for writing a very free version of only some of it. That he attaches more importance to this type later in his life does not reflect some quirk on his part, but reveals a real understanding of the essence of sonata style.

It was observed before [p. 87] that Haydn sometimes re-uses thematic elements throughout the exposition; for example, in some cases the first thematic element of the first group is the first of the second group, and even of the transition too. He sometimes goes further by deriving entirely new matter from the same figures, as in the first movement of the *String Quarted in C major Hob.III:77*. If in the recapitulation there were a repeat of the exposition with the same thematic element regardless of its texture three or more times in the tonic key, plus what might occur in the coda, the result would be utterly tiresome, and far worse than repeating different musical matter entirely in the tonic. Haydn was well aware of the dangers and came up with an admirable solution to the problem.

In order to understand what that solution was, one must listen carefully to the type of musical matter found in those free recapitulations. Two types are clear. One is statement matter; the other is unmistakably termination matter. None of it is development matter, as has sometimes been suggested, because it does not grow and transform itself, especially tonally, as development matter does. The statement matter is usually confined to the first group in full at the beginning of the recapitulation, the last statement of the exposition further along and before what would be designated as the coda. In the first movement of his *Symphony in G major Hob.I:92*, mm.21-39[8] recur as mm.125-143 and mm.72-81 as mm.191-200. Mm.145 and 181 embrace the free passage, and the coda begins at m.200.

---

[8]The *Allegro* begins at m.21.

Example V:11

end First

<hr />

⁹To the question, "Does this first group modulate to the dominant?" the answer must be "No!," because the apparent change of key is not backed up by the use of the secondary dominant, and the dominant key is not retained

143 Group[9]

Part of first statement, minor.
Free Passage

G minor

Falling chromatic scale to m.153

151

G major restored

into m.143. And furthermore, the dominant key is not wanted at this point in the recapitulation. (See also m.39 in the exposition. *Example II:4*)

Tonal inflexion →

Sec. domt.
of G major

Part of first statement, major

G major

cf. mm.51-6

180: First Group matter joined to Transition matter from mm.33 & 51

187

Last Exposition statement from m.72

Exposition's
termination matter

Coda
Transition
matter

194

Part of first statement

Significant conflict

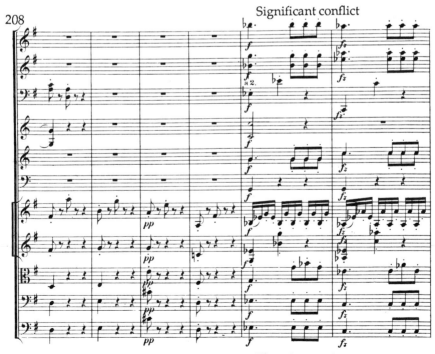

Eb major tonal standpoint

dim. 7th as
sec. domt.

G major

Part of first statement

Part of last
exposition statement

226

The 'free passage' begins at m.145 on the tonic minor, reverts to the major at m.155, which is inflected by sequence through mm.159-165, but which remains firmly in the major to m.181. None of the musical matter in this free passage is sufficient in length to be designated as statement, and its effect is what one would expect to find in a coda. That is, it is termination matter.

It is not until m.212 that Haydn takes his first plunge into deep conflict within the recapitulation/coda, though there is the intrusion of the tonic minor at m.144, the tonal inflection of mm.160-165, and the textural and thematic contrasts throughout. He does it simply to establish a point from which he can rebound out of the movement. The tonal standpoint is E-flat major, the flat-sixth of G major. This is fairly typical of the approach to the coda from the mid-late 1780s onwards.

Exercise 32

Compare the exposition and recapitulation/coda of the first movement of one of these works by Haydn:
    Symphony in G major 'Paukenschlag' Hob.I:94
    String Quartet in D minor Hob.III:76

B: Coda

As previously stated [p. 32], a piece of music does not just end; it is finished off. This is done in the last section of the movement known as the coda. Sometimes the coda is no more than the kind of cadential formula described on p. 32. In lighter sonatas it might be exactly the same as the termination found at the end of the exposition, because there is sufficient conclusiveness in those measures. Sometimes a little more is required. Compare the end of the first movement of Beethoven's *Pianoforte Sonata in F minor op.2 no.1* with the end of its exposition in *Example I:24*.

Example V:12

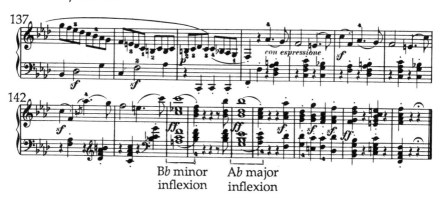

Bb minor · Ab major
inflexion · inflexion

Beethoven chose to heighten the effect by inflecting mm.146-147 towards the subdominant (B-flat minor), then the mediant (A-flat major), followed by a sequence of chords retaining the falling fifth in the melody and accentuated *sforzando* on the off-beat. This supplement to the exposition's termination is little other than a sequential extension of the cadence of mm.47-48 accelerated to the final cadence.

Due to their scale and length some movements do need a long coda in order to achieve a stable termination. This is not done by merely restating a number of thematic elements from earlier in the movement, revamped or not, in the tonic key. Such a procedure would be as ineffective through its monotony as a recapitulation entirely in the tonic. A device that is often adopted is a very prominent tonal shift to a remote tonal standpoint from the end of the recapitulation to the beginning of the coda, and in association with a significant theme, especially the first. The music is then allowed to go forward from there. The propulsive effect of this device is enormous.

In the first movement of Beethoven's *Pianoforte Sonata in C major op.53* the coda begins on D-flat major; in the first movement of the *Eroica Symphony no.3 in E-flat major op.55* on C major; and in the first movement of his *Symphony no.8 in F major op.93* on D-flat major. In each case Beethoven moves on from the new tonal standpoint, not in a developmental manner, despite the fragmentation of the themes, but through a modulatory chord progression back to the tonic key. The approach to each of these three keys is through a very individual type of transition in the case of *Opus 53* and *Opus 93* and through juxtaposed chords in *Opus 55*. All three must be classified as transition matter. Of course, this causes a serious point of conflict; but it is the preceding transition and not the termination itself that causes it. Such a deep point of conflict at the start of the coda acts like a coiled spring. The composer must let the music recoil from such a position quickly then go forward to the end of the movement without any further disturbance. This ensures a complete sense of resolution to the movement.

Exercise 33

Compare some movements which end with the same termination matter as the exposition with others that have an additional coda. Comment on the characteristics of the construction in each case, and assess the effectiveness of the resolution it brings about.

Exercise 34

Examine the coda of a major movement where the coda begins with a tonal standpoint remote from the tonic, and assess its role in resolving all previous conflicts.

Exercise 35

Explain the *fortissimo* C-sharp in m.17 of the last movement of Beethoven's Eighth Symphony in the context of the whole movement.

Conclusion

Music is, *par excellence*, both an art and a science. As an art it expresses some of the most deeply felt and ineffable human emotions; as a science it is a process of thought that has its own inherent logic. As an art it can be viewed as reflecting the broad changes that take place in humankind and its society; as a science it has parallels with the developing logic of other intellectual activities, such as mathematics, theoretical physics, formal logic and architecture. Just as society undergoes processes of evolution and change for diverse reasons, just as discoveries in other activities usually render earlier patterns of thought inapplicable or invalid, so too are discoveries made that keep music in a state of constant change. Thus musical styles and forms are never absolutes, but are a reflection of the state of musical thought at particular times.

Having stated this, it must be emphasized that, like all human thought and artistic activity, music does not move ahead in straight lines, but is subject to extensive bifurcation. Its progress is not regular, but is erratic; nor is it uniform, since many composers who lack the imagination and creativity of their brighter and more perceptive contemporaries tend to cling to the past. The social circumstances that might accompany its progress are always uneven, for reasons that can usually be traced to political, social or religious attitudes and the level of economic prosperity. It seems that the *avant garde* flourishes best where circumstances combine to form the strongest catalyst for the reaction of genius and ideas.

The subject of this book is one of the more prominent examples of the duality of unfolding musical thought and the progression of human development. The main purpose has been to explain, as simply as possible with such a complex subject, the principles of sonata form through its clearest manifestation during the period 1785-1810. A comprehensive history covering the hundred years of its occurrence is a topic for a separate book. Yet to understand sonata form fully, its ancestry cannot be ignored.

One of the more misguided and irritating arguments that has pervaded twentieth century analysis is whether theme design or tonality caused the change from early eighteenth century style to late eighteenth century style. The fact is that neither was a greater cause than the other. Composers worked them both in tandem with each other and with texture. In order to apprehend the stages by which late eighteenth century style evolved, it is necessary not to conduct chicken-and-egg arguments for or against the precedence of theme design or tonality, nor to look at total structure as a generality, but instead to examine the detailed characteristics of musical matter. It is from the relationships of different types of matter that the total structure grows; and it was only through the composers' grasp of how to devise and manipulate the different types of matter that the essence of sonata style became more prominent as the period wore on.

Of the five types of musical matter described in Chapter 1, statement was the one that yielded the first fruits of the composers' attention. While it is not possible, for lack of reliable dating, to establish a chronology for a sufficient body of the repertoire or to discuss what is available in print in great detail here, it is clear that by the 1720s a radical re-designing of statement matter found in orchestral music and operatic arias was well underway. The principal focus of attention was the detailed design of phrases and sub-phrases, and particularly the dimension of the smallest components of the phrase. But when did each one of the types of statement described in Chapter 1 [pp.17-22] emerge? And by what stages did each one develop? As was pointed out [p.17] *alternatim* statements occur throughout the sonata period. A very early and no more than seminal example occupies the opening measures of the Italian-style Sinfonia to Francesco Bartolomeo Conti's oratorio, *La colpa originale*,[1] which is dated around 1718-1725.

Example VI:1

___
[1]Hermine W. Williams, Italians in Vienna, *The Symphony 1720-1840*, Ser.B, Vol.II; New York and London, Garland Publishing (1983).

Mm.1-12 are repeated exactly at the end of the movement with one cadence measure added. There can be little doubt that this type was one of the major factors in introducing the idea of conflict through juxtaposition into musical style. Further, the sudden change at m.22 to the second violin's sixteenth notes, which give a bustle prophetic of a late eighteenth century transition, is another factor.

The three types of matter that most influenced the growth of this idea were transition, preparation and development. While conflict can and does occur within statement, it is controlled by these three, with the control exercised through the manipulation of their textural, thematic and tonal elements. As the sonata period proceeded, the function of each of these types of matter became ever more distinctive.

Around 1750 the best development usually amounted to no more than a phrase twice or thrice stated in stepwise rising sequence, followed by a passage that made way for the return of the tonic.

Example VI:2

---

[2]The use of the tonic key here can be attributed to the fact that the exposition is not repeated.

∟ Row of 7th chords ⌐
See Ex. IV:7

m.92 = Recapitulation

In this example from Johann Stamitz's *Symphony in E-flat major*[3] the sequence of mm.78-84 is clear, and its harmonic structure is cleverly fluid. There follow several measures of harmonic progression, in which there is no significant tonal standpoint. A comparison might be made between the role of these measures and mm.112-141 of the first movement of Beethoven's *Pianoforte Sonata in C major op.53*. [see *Example IV:6*] The principle is the same; only the scale is different. Stamitz deliberately confuses the tonality so that the tonic key that follows can provide a significant point of resolution.

The *Symphony in D major* of 1746 by Georg Christoph Wagenseil[4] does it rather differently.

---

[3]Hugo Riemann (ed), *Mannheim Symphonists: A Collection of Twenty-four Orchestral Works*; (Rpt.) New York: Broude Brothers (n.d.) Vol. I, 36.

[4]*Denkmäler der Tonkunst in Österreich*, Band 31, 16.

Example VI:3

Here the development section comprises the phrase of mm.2-3, first on A major then on B minor, though beginning on the half-measure. What follows can be described as fairly orthodox preparation, which leads to the recapitulation at m.44.

The development matter of the above examples is different from the sequential treatment of figures that is found in the music in early eighteenth century style. When sequences occur there, they are less harmonically unstable and have only a modulatory function. The above type of sequence serves to create conflict through its harmonic instability and dramatic texture. And further, where in the early eighteenth century style a passage in sequence occurs, it is not followed by preparation matter or the total tonal instability found in the Stamitz example.

In the early days of sonata form, transition matter was no more than a straight-forward modulatory passage that emerged from the first statement and merged into the second. In some small scale movements it was dispensed with altogether, and the first and second statements and their keys were merely juxtaposed. Where there is a transition, it is often so closely dovetailed that separating it from the first and second groups is as impossible as it is for the first movement of Beethoven's *Pianoforte Sonata in A major op.101*. The first movement of the Wagenseil symphony is a case in point, and for that reason the example is left without annotation.

Example VI:4

The separation of the transition from the first and second groups and its evolution into the types described in *Chapter 3* [pp. 62-66] took several decades; but, it was a very important factor in delineating the shape of sonata form and in stimulating the invention of another type of musical matter.

Finally comes the question of termination matter. The earliest codas, where they exist at all, were no more than a repetition of the tonic chord for one measure. The enlargement of that measure into a substantial section of the movement with its own type of matter was another process that spread itself over several decades. The evolution of what occurs at the end of the movement is to some extent related to that which occurs at the end of the exposition.

Historians have been wont to describe the music of the hundred years of sonata style by the terms *galant, rococco, Empfindsamkeit, Sturm und Drang* and *classical*. With these terms, whether valid or not, they have intended to reflect different currents or trends within that period. But a much more fundamental view of the aesthetics of sonata style can be suggested. In his well-known *Essay on the True Art of Playing Keyboard Instruments*[5] *C.P.E. Bach explained:*

> A musician cannot move others unless he too is moved. He must of necessity feel all of the affects that he hopes to arouse in his audience ... In languishing, sad passages, the performer must languish and grow sad ... Similarly, in lively, joyous passages, the executant must again put himself into the appropriate mood. And so, constantly varying the passions, he will barely quiet one before he rouses another.

Now, it was recognized by the generation preceding C.P.E. Bach that a single composition or movement would have only one *affectus* or emotional state. From that practice the Theory of Affects (*Affektenlehre*) evolved. Consideration of a few different pieces of music in early eighteenth century style should persuade one of the merit of that theory.

The above words of C.P.E. Bach suggest that he had recognized not later than 1753 that a piece of music could have more than one *affectus*. As he was discussing performance, not composition, he did not go so far as to state that a piece of music must have more than one *affectus*. But again, consideration of a few works in sonata style will be persuasive enough.

Any study of the history of sonata style must not begin with the possible existence of currents or trends that might be labelled by the terms used above. It must begin on the premise that the compositional practice of the early eighteenth century summarized in the Theory of Affects was supplanted by a new practice, in which the *affectus* changed from passage to passage. The approach to this study must be a technical one, identifying when each type of musical matter found in sonata style began to emerge and when they began to distinguish themselves clearly one from another. This must be related to the increasing contrast of *affectus*. One thing will be found. In many works contrasting *affectus* are juxtaposed. This is especially obvious at the conjunction of the end of the transition and the start of the second group. Yet by Beethoven's time the music was composed so that the *affectus* often surged from one to another. Inevitably, in the long process of working out the essence of sonata style there were different currents and trends. These must not be viewed as the idea itself, but as aspects of the idea. That idea was the logical evolution of musical thought, which is in a curious way a reflection of the evolution of humankind and its society at that time.

---

[5]translated and edited by William J. Mitchell; London: Eulenburg (1974) 152.

Index of Works Cited

Beethoven, Ludwig van
    Pianoforte Sonatas

op.2, no.1:	22, 32, 82, 90, 146
op.2, no.2:	64-5
op.2, no.3:	22, 32-3, 35, 72, 90, 127
Op.7:	65-6, 72, 90
op.10, no.1:	26, 29-30, 74-5, 90, 92-4, 131
op.10, no.2:	64, 114
op.10, no.3:	13-4
op.13:	83-5, 87, 131
op.14, no.1:	7, 23-5, 62, 115-6
op.14, no.2:	23-5, 65
op.22	12, 63
op.28:	53-4
op.31, no.1:	12
op.31, no.2:	42-3, 61, 90
op.31, no.3:	61-2, 70-2
op.53:	10-2, 15-6, 34, 41-2, 72, 90, 98-102, 106, 123-5, 146-7
op.57:	87, 125
op.81a:	33-4
op.101:	89
op.106:	22, 58-60, 101

    String Quartet op.18, no.4: 25-6, 66, 72, 126-7

    Symphonies

1:	28-9, 30
2:	10, 30
3:	22, 57, 60, 86, 127-31, 146-7
4:	50-3
5:	13-4, 18-21
8:	30-1, 146-7
9:	61

Conti, Francesco Bartolomeo
    Sinfonia, *La copla originale* 150-2

Haydn, Franz Joseph
    Pianoforte Sonatas
        Hob.XVI:23: 13
        Hob.XVI:28-7: 26-7